Praise for *Our Common*

"Jonathan Rowe's work off   'ings new depths of common se   , and social crises of our world. Who knew that there could be such a marriage of hope and hard-hitting clarity!"

—Jacob Needleman, author of *An Unknown World*

"Read this book as though you were opening a treasure chest. It transcends our stale left-right debates and reveals the wealth available to all of us if we just recognize and protect it."

—Sarah van Gelder, Executive Editor, *YES! Magazine*

"I've met a lot of people in my life but none quite like my friend Jonathan Rowe. He was a unique and original thinker who constantly challenged our prevailing ideas of progress."

—Byron Dorgan, former US Senator

"This brilliant book by a wonderful man we lost too soon illuminates the essential question of our politics going forward: are we all in this together? Jonathan Rowe's answer is a resounding and convincing *yes!*"

—Jonathan Alter, NBC news analyst and author of *The Promise: President Obama, Year One*

"Most journalists leave behind nothing more than ephemeral news clips about forgotten but overhyped crises. Jonathan Rowe bequeathed to us a provocative concept that could unite left and right—the fostering of places and institutions outside the realms of business and government that can protect us from twenty-first-century avarice."

—Walter Shapiro, veteran political columnist

"Jonathan Rowe maps out a vast swath of our economy that few of us have considered and conventional economists have persistently failed to account for—the cooperative realms of family, neighborhoods, and civic society. The relentless colonization of these realms by the market explains much that has gone wrong with modern society."

—Paul Glastris, Editor in Chief, *Washington Monthly*

"If there is any way out of the squeeze that afflicts today's economy, it will partly be through the ideas held in this book. And Rowe delineates them with both a philosopher's eye and a poet's touch. Rarely has the potential of the commons been explained so clearly."

—Todd Oppenheimer, author of *The Flickering Mind*

"Jonathan Rowe was a modern-day Johnny Appleseed, happily planting practical ideas that others missed or dismissed. In *Our Common Wealth*, he shows how we can share, rather than destroy, the varied bounties of our earth and our own communities."

—Russ Baker, Editor, *WhoWhatWhy*

"Jonathan Rowe creates a whole new entry in the tired national debate between state and market: the commons. His thinking is neither liberal nor conservative—the commons must be protected from the state as well as from corporations. This is a beautiful little book."

—Mickey Kaus, author of *The End of Equality*

"*Our Common Wealth* is a vitally important book that lights the way to putting economics in the service of human needs."

—Gregg Easterbrook, author of *The Leading Indicators*

"*Our Common Wealth* delivers a jolt of common sense. This book is Jonathan Rowe's legacy as *Small Is Beautiful* is E. F. Schumacher's."

—Jay Walljasper, author of *All That We Share*

"Many modern readers still appreciate Montaigne's timeless essays. I fully expect citizens of future centuries to discover—and similarly appreciate—Jonathan's remarkable insights and wisdom, too."

—Phil Keisling, Director, Center for Public Service, Portland State University

"Jon Rowe's genius lay in understanding the nature of shared wealth and the taking of that wealth. Pure air is wealth we share; air pollution is a taking of that wealth. Contemplative quiet is shared wealth; noise pollution is a taking of it. What makes life worth living is common wealth—public health, community, nature, privacy, access to knowledge, the joys of childhood, thousands of things we hardly notice. There is an economics of common wealth. Common wealth can and must be managed. That is Jon Rowe's message to us."

—George Lakoff, Professor of Cognitive Science and Linguistics, University of California, Berkeley, and author of *Don't Think of an Elephant*

"No one understands the depth and beauty of the commons better than Jonathan Rowe did, and none have expressed it as clearly. The best of his writing on the subject is in your hands. It will change your take on just about everything."

—Mark Dowie, investigative journalist

"Jonathan Rowe had an enviable gift for stripping complex ideas down to their essence. No idea mattered more to him than preserving the things we all share free of charge against the encroachments of capitalism. This jewel of a book describes how the commons sustains and enriches our lives and what we can do to save it."

—Timothy Noah, author of *The Great Divergence*

"Jonathan Rowe has bequeathed a book to us that does nothing less than make the invisible visible. After reading its crystal-clear pages, you will redouble your efforts to protect the things that matter most."

—Alan AtKisson, author of *The Sustainability Transformation*

"This profoundly sensible and humane book is the perfect antidote to selfishness, greed, and the mindless pursuit of profit that endangers even the air we breathe."

—Charles Peters, Founding Editor, *Washington Monthly*

"In both his writing and his life, Jonathan Rowe was the explorer, cartographer, and defender of the commons. This book illuminates the ways in which the commons provides a framework for all of economics."

—Edgar Cahn, founder, TimeBanks USA

"Jonathan Rowe never shied away from an idea because it was too big, too new, or too unlikely to be taken seriously. He believed the world could be changed for the better if we look beyond clichéd notions."

—Sam Smith, Editor, *The Progressive Review*

"Jonathan Rowe was an artist with words, a craftsman who wrote with the kind of care he saw disappearing from our hurried, consumer-centered society. While no book can do full justice to his life and thought, this one gives us a wonderful glimpse into them."

—John de Graaf, coauthor of *What's the Economy For, Anyway?* and *Affluenza*

OUR COMMON WEALTH

ALSO BY JONATHAN ROWE

Time Dollars
(with Edgar Cahn)

OUR COMMON WEALTH

The Hidden Economy That Makes Everything Else Work

■ ■ ■

JONATHAN ROWE

Edited by Peter Barnes
Foreword by Bill McKibben
Afterword by David Bollier

BK

Berrett–Koehler Publishers, Inc.
San Francisco
a BK Currents book

COPYRIGHT © 2013 BY JONATHAN ROWE

All rights reserved. No part of this publication may be reproduced, distributed, or transmitted in any form or by any means, including photocopying, recording, or other electronic or mechanical methods, without the prior written permission of the publisher, except in the case of brief quotations embodied in critical reviews and certain other noncommercial uses permitted by copyright law. For permission requests, write to the publisher, addressed "Attention: Permissions Coordinator," at the address below.

Berrett-Koehler Publishers, Inc.
235 Montgomery Street, Suite 650, San Francisco, CA 94104-2916
Tel: (415) 288-0260   Fax: (415) 362-2512   www.bkconnection.com

ORDERING INFORMATION

Quantity sales. Special discounts are available on quantity purchases by corporations, associations, and others. For details, contact the "Special Sales Department" at the Berrett-Koehler address above.

Individual sales. Berrett-Koehler publications are available through most bookstores. They can also be ordered directly from Berrett-Koehler: Tel: (800) 929-2929; Fax: (802) 864-7626; www.bkconnection.com

Orders for college textbook/course adoption use. Please contact Berrett-Koehler: Tel: (800) 929-2929; Fax: (802) 864-7626.

Orders by U.S. trade bookstores and wholesalers. Please contact Ingram Publisher Services, Tel: (800) 509-4887; Fax: (800) 838-1149; E-mail: customer.service@ingrampublisher services .com; or visit www.ingrampublisherservices.com/Ordering for details about electronic ordering.

Berrett-Koehler and the BK logo are registered trademarks of Berrett-Koehler Publishers, Inc.

PRINTED IN THE UNITED STATES OF AMERICA

Berrett-Koehler books are printed on long-lasting acid-free paper. When it is available, we choose paper that has been manufactured by environmentally responsible processes. These may include using trees grown in sustainable forests, incorporating recycled paper, minimizing chlorine in bleaching, or recycling the energy produced at the paper mill.

LIBRARY OF CONGRESS CATALOGING-IN-PUBLICATION DATA

Rowe, Jonathan.
Our common wealth : the hidden economy that makes everything else work
/ by Jonathan Rowe ; edited by Peter Barnes ; foreword by Bill McKibben ;
afterword by David Bollier.
   pages cm
Includes bibliographical references.
ISBN 978-1-60994-833-7 (pbk.)
 1. Commons. 2. Cooperation. 3. Economics. I. Barnes, Peter, 1942–
II. Title.
HD1286.R69 2013
330--dc23
                    2012039496

FIRST EDITION

18 17 16 15 14 13   10 9 8 7 6 5 4 3 2 1

INTERIOR DESIGN/ART: Valerie Brewster   EDIT: Thalia Publishing Services
COVER/JACKET DESIGN: M.80 / Wes Youssi   PROOFREAD: Henri Bensussen
COVER/JACKET ILLUSTRATION: © Gary Alphonso/www.i2iart.com
PRODUCTION SERVICE: Linda Jupiter Productions   INDEX: Linda Webster

For Josh and Mary Jean

CONTENTS

Ill fares the land,
to hastening ills a prey,
where wealth accumulates,
and men decay.

OLIVER GOLDSMITH (1770)

■ ■ ■

A proper community . . . is a commonwealth: a place,
a resource, an economy. It answers the needs, practical as well as social and spiritual, of its members —
among them the need to need one another.

WENDELL BERRY (1987)

■ ■ ■

FOREWORD

by Bill McKibben

I n case you think there's anything small or secondary about
the idea of the commons, in case you think it a molehill to
the mountain of our economy, consider the issue that lies
athwart our progress as a civilization: climate change.

One economist after another has described climate change
as a "market failure," the greatest of all time, since without a
price attached to use of the atmosphere we continue to pollute it with abandon. But the solution to climate change
requires us to understand that the atmosphere is a commons.
If it belongs to anyone, it belongs to all of us. And if Exxon
and other fossil fuel companies want to use it as a dump, they
need to compensate us at a rate that leads to the rapid tech-
nological and social change on which our future depends.

Our greatest climatologist, James Hansen, the man who
first alerted the world to the crisis, has led a relentless

campaign for just this response, terming it "fee-and-dividend." So it's not too much to say that our future as a species requires grasping the ideas in this book.

Which is why it's so good that Jon Rowe was perhaps the clearest writer I can think of. In these chapters he manages to take a concept most people have never really considered and put it in terms that no reasonable reader will reject. This is especially telling because the subset of the population that has heard of the commons has usually heard of it in negative terms.

Garrett Hardin's famous essay, "The Tragedy of the Commons," was, as it turned out, both seductively appealing and almost entirely wrong. As Rowe demonstrates, communities around the planet have managed to hold land and many other things in common, and to do so wisely and carefully. It's only when those commons are invaded by a rampaging market that their protective arrangements break down. We've wasted a good many years following Hardin's libertarian solutions. Now it's time to get on a workable path.

As we do, it's worth underlining that there's nothing automatic about managing a successful commons. It requires us to be in contact, and to think about how we fit into the greater whole. It asks us to be more than mere consumers. And as Rowe points out again and again, we're completely capable of doing that. This is evident not just in olden-day stories about pastures, but in up-to-the-minute tales of Wikipedia, land trusts, public radio, and farmer's markets.

In the past year, the Occupy movement has limned the failures of our market economy. Many have complained, however, that Occupy didn't come up with a set of solutions. In fact, the commons in its many guises is the end to which their outrage points (and even, in the self-government of the Occupy encampments, what it began to model).

THE COMMONS DOESN'T CONSTITUTE THE WHOLE answer; there are many things markets do well, as long as they're adequately regulated. But it is the ideas in this book that point the way forward. Jon Rowe, a wise and decent man and a good friend, died much too soon. He's not here to lead the charge, so we need to spread his insights together.

Bill McKibben is an author, climate activist, and Schumann Distinguished Scholar at Middlebury College. He has written more than a dozen books, including The End of Nature *(1989) and* Eaarth: Making a Life on a Tough New Planet *(2010). He currently leads the climate campaigning organization 350.org.*

Introduction

As Highway 1 winds north from San Francisco along the Pacific coast, a rusty road sign proclaims, "Point Reyes Station—Population 350." That's an understatement these days, but it aptly reflects the way Jonathan Rowe, who lived here for the last decade of his life, thought about the town. Sure, parking is sometimes hard to find on Main Street and the feed barn now includes an espresso bar, but Point Reyes Station is still a very quiet place, nestled amid nature and farms, with friendly merchants, a local newspaper (two, actually), and caring neighbors. Which is how Jonathan Rowe thought the world ought to be.

I met Jonathan long before either of us lived here. We first connected in Washington in the 1970s when I was a reporter for *The New Republic* and he, a recent law school graduate, was among Ralph Nader's first "Raiders." We clicked instantly and remained close friends (and eventually neighbors) until his sudden death in 2011.

Jonathan was a brilliant, complex, and somewhat quirky man. Other adjectives that could be applied to him include humble, deeply religious (in the best sense), and loving. He was both a thinker and a doer, with each activity enriching the other. And he was a wonderful, almost poetic, storyteller. He made his graceful paragraphs seem effortless, though of course they never were.

Jonathan grew up in small towns on Cape Cod. The arc of his life flowed through Boston, Washington, New York, and San Francisco, with a detour through Philadelphia, but his small-town roots never left him. After Nader he worked for a mayor of Washington (Marion Barry) and a U. S. Senator (Byron Dorgan of North Dakota). He wrote for the *Christian Science Monitor*, the *Washington Monthly*, the *Atlantic Monthly*, and many other journals. His achievements are too numerous to list here, but one is worth special note: his slow and difficult ascent from stutterer to radio talk show host.

Intellectually, Jonathan journeyed too. At Harvard in the 1960s he was a Goldwater Republican. Gradually and somewhat reluctantly, he shifted to the left. Yet all his life he retained the temperament of a Burkean conservative, and one of his great disappointments was seeing the conservative movement taken over by billionaires, yahoos, and zealots. His writings covered many subjects. What unified them were lifelong preferences for small over big, local over distant, and nonmonetary over monetary relationships. These were the source of his passion for the commons.

Jonathan was what you might call a *scalist*, someone who thinks scale is really important, possibly more important than anything else, and that there are such things as *enough* and *too much*. Eat one cheeseburger and you feel great, eat two and you're stuffed, eat three and you're sick. The optimal scale for a human community is substantially greater than one, but never greater than the number of people who can sort of know each other, or so Jonathan thought. Similarly, the optimal quantity of many sorts of human activity is far short of infinity, yet we seemingly don't know when or how to slow down.

Jonathan didn't discover, or more precisely, name, the commons until late in his life. In the mid-1990s he moved to San Francisco to work with a now-defunct think tank called Redefining Progress. The group's premise was that what mainstream economists call "progress" is in fact the opposite. Since the 1970s, the think tank argued, economic growth in the United States has led to less happiness, not more. In this spirit, Jonathan lead-authored a much-discussed *Atlantic Monthly* article called "If the GDP Is Up, Why Is America Down?"[1] The group's remedies for this dissonance were better economic indicators (down with GDP!) and taxes on "bads" like pollution instead of "goods" like labor.

Such remedies were not entirely satisfying to Jonathan; they felt more technical than human. What Jonathan wanted was to revivify a whole spectrum of human activity that was small, local, and mostly nonmonetary. He knew such activity was widespread, but it didn't have a name. After much thought, he stuck an old but appropriate tag on it: "the commons." Once he took this leap, a whole world opened up.

JONATHAN'S FIRST ARTICLE MENTIONING "THE COMMONS" was published in 2001 in *The American Prospect*.[2] It was not about the commons per se, but about a time banking system invented by his friend Edgar Cahn. (See chapter 18, "Time Banking.") In the system, members of a community provide services for each other at no cost. For each hour members help one another, they get credit recorded in a computer that they can draw on when they need help themselves. In the article Jonathan traced the system's roots to colonial days when settlers built cohesive communities around a common pasture.

Soon Jonathan had constructed a larger narrative that saw the commons as a collection of many shared natural and social assets, including the Earth's ecosystems, the ecologies of small communities, the Internet, and our collective achievements in a myriad of fields. This is a much larger vision of the commons than we are accustomed to. In it, the commons is a vast economic realm, comparable in scale to the market and just as important. "It is a parallel economy that does real work," Jonathan would write later, "a counterpoise to the market that provides antidotes to many pathologies of the modern age." Moreover, this broadly conceived commons is far from being a relic; in fact, it is needed today more than ever. "At the start of the industrial age, products were scarce and commons abundant. All the gears were arranged to produce more stuff. But times change and scarcities shift. Where once the products of the market were scarce, now it is commons that are scarce and also most needed."

What unifies this extremely diverse sector are its operating principles. Unlike the market, which is organized to maximize short-term private gain, the commons is (or should be) organized to preserve shared assets for future generations and to spread their benefits more or less equally among the living. If government nurtured this sector as zealously as it nurtures the market, the modern world would be a healthier and happier place.

Along with David Bollier, Harriet Barlow, Julie Ristau, and myself, Jonathan cofounded the Tomales Bay Institute (named for a bay near Point Reyes Station) that later became a network called On The Commons. Together we cranked out reports and articles making the case for the commons piece by piece and as an entirety. In doing this work Jonathan pulled together all of his lifelong thinking. In his mind he'd finally found, if not a panacea, at least an antidote to the numerous failings of the market.

During these years Jonathan settled into small-town life again and started a family. He married Mary Jean Espulgar, a Filipina he met in San Francisco, and they had a son, Josh. Jonathan walked Josh to school every day, coached Little League baseball, helped the local newspapers and radio station, made countless friends, and was probably happier than at any time in his life. He also became familiar with village life in the Philippines and drew many lessons from that.

As always, he strove to combine practice with theory. With Elizabeth Barnet, he cofounded a group called West Marin Commons, which among other things created a town square, or *zócalo*, out of an empty lot, a community garden of native plants, and a website for sharing free stuff. This was of a piece with his fondness for traditional Main Streets and neighborhoods with places to sit. He also reported on local commons' efforts across America—farmers' markets, land trusts, municipal wi-fi networks, open spaces for pedestrians and bench-sitters, websites for sharing things, and so on. These stories convinced him that a commons movement is stirring, even if the stirrers don't know it yet.

While the focus of Jonathan's writing and engagement was local, he was fully aware of the larger-scale problems humanity faces. He appreciated that while informal, participatory commons work well in small communities and online, they are insufficient to deal with corporate power, environmental degradation, and extreme inequality. Bigger and more structured institutions are needed for those challenges.

To address these systemic problems Jonathan envisioned an assortment of trusts empowered to protect large commons from corporate invasion. Just as corporations are legally bound to protect the interests of their shareholders, so the trusts would be legally obliged to preserve the commons under their charge. To do this effectively, the lawyer in Jonathan understood, they'd need strong property rights, including the rights to charge rent and pay dividends to owners. "Put commoners in charge of the air, let us charge polluters for using it, and we'll see a lot less pollution than we do now," he wrote.

What particularly excited Jonathan about the commons is its potential to realign American politics. Jonathan himself was what linguist George Lakoff calls a "bi-conceptual"— he harbored conservative as well as liberal tendencies and was able to live with both. Because the commons is distinct from both the state and the market, Jonathan saw it as a way to bridge left and right. This may seem quixotic, but just the other night, as I watched Fox News at an airport, I heard right-wing commentator Bill O'Reilly opine with fervor (after blaming President Obama for high oil prices) that "we the people own the gas and oil discovered in America. It's our land and the government administers it in our name." Like-minded pundit Lou Dobbs then pitched a national version of the Alaska Permanent Fund that would return part of the value of America's oil as dividends to every citizen.[3]

In the end, what Jonathan wanted was not a world without markets or profit-seeking businesses—that would be absurd— but a world in which markets and commons live in symbiosis. "The goal isn't to replace the market with the commons but to build a durable balance between them."

THE BOOK THAT FOLLOWS WAS WRITTEN IN BITS AND pieces between 1993 and 2011. If Jonathan had lived he would have finished it with more grace than I have. Under the circumstances, I've done what I could. I pored through Jonathan's writings about the commons and tried to extract and blend the best. In doing this I edited ever-so-lightly to avoid repetition, bring up to date, and shape a symphony out of melodies composed years apart.

Like any fine writer, Jonathan would surely have quibbled with some of my edits, but I believe he'd be pleased with the book as a whole. It captures his thoughts, spirit, and style. It puts, as Jonathan did, roughly equal weight on theory and practice. And it makes a rousing case, as only Jonathan could, for defending, revitalizing, sharing, and preserving the wealth that is the ultimate source of our well-being and that rightfully belongs to all of us.

Peter Barnes
Point Reyes Station, California
November 2012

THEORY

There is a body of thought surrounding the commons, and there are efforts in the real world to strengthen the commons. The first part of the book focuses on the former, the second on the latter. In short, theory and practice.

Rowe begins by painting a picture of the commons in the twenty-first century. This picture goes well beyond the familiar one from medieval Europe; it is shared wealth writ large. It includes innumerable gifts of nature and society, from the atmosphere to the Internet, science to children's stories, soil to community strength. We inherit these assets jointly and hold them in trust, morally if not legally, for those who come after us. These assets are essential to human and planetary well-being as well as to the functioning of our modern economy. Yet to economists and others, they are stunningly invisible.

Economists fail to see the commons because its contributions are difficult to monetize. They also don't believe that humans can act on impulses other than self-gain. Disregard of the commons was also spurred by biologist Garrett Hardin's essay, "The Tragedy of the Commons," which holds that commons are inherently self-destructive. Rowe shows that, to the contrary, commons are quite capable of sustaining themselves when protected from predatory forces. The real tragedy is not that commons self-destruct but that they are devoured by outside profit-seekers.

Rowe offers a new story of the commons not as tragedy but as shared wealth under siege. The story identifies both the value of the wealth and its foes. The value of the commons lies not only in the services it provides—a stable climate, a sense of belonging, a vast store of knowledge—but also in its ability to temper the market's mindless profit-maximizing that distorts so much around us. The foes of the commons change over time, but nowadays are mostly privatizing corporations.

To protect the commons against privatizers, Rowe suggests we deploy a toolset not usually associated with the commons: property rights. At the moment, property rights protect private wealth much more than common wealth, but that could change. New common property rights—and common property-owning institutions such as trusts—could defend the commons against incursion and ensure that they are preserved for the long term.

In the last chapter of this part, Rowe notes that traditional conservatives understood that markets need limits, just as the state does. He laments that in recent decades, that kind of conservatism has been displaced by a more cynical kind that believes it is okay to waste our patrimony so long as somebody makes money doing it.

—*Ed.*

1

Our Hidden Wealth

My wife grew up in what Western experts, not without condescension, call a "developing" country. The social life of her village revolved largely around a tree. People gathered there in the evening to visit, tell stories, or just pass the time. Some of my wife's warmest childhood memories are of playing hide-and-seek late into the evening while adults chatted under the tree.

The tree was more than a quaint meeting place; it was an economic asset in the root sense of that word. It produced a bonding of neighbors, an information network, an activity center for kids, and a bridge between generations. Older people could be part of the flow of daily life, and children got to experience something scarce in the United States today—an unstructured and noncompetitive setting in which their parents were close at hand.

In the United States we spend hundreds of billions of dollars on everything from community centers to kiddie videos to try to achieve those results, with great inefficiency and often much less positive effect. Yet most Western economists would regard the tree as a pathetic state of underdevelopment. They would urge "modernization," by which they would mean cutting down the tree and making people pay money for what it provided. In their preferred vision, corporate-produced entertainment would displace local culture. Something free and available to all would become commodities sold for a price. The result would be "growth" as economists understand that term.

That's the story of *the commons*, a generic term (like *the market* and *the state*) that denotes wealth we share. To use this term is to evoke a puzzled pause. You mean the government? The common people? That park in Boston? In fact, the commons includes our entire life support system, both natural and social. The air and oceans, the web of species, wilderness and flowing water—all are parts of the commons. So are language and knowledge, sidewalks and public squares, the stories of childhood, the processes of democracy. Some parts of the commons are gifts of nature, others the product of human endeavor. Some are new, such as the Internet; others are as ancient as soil and calligraphy.

What they have in common is that they all "belong" to all of us, if that is the word. No one has exclusive rights to them. We inherit them jointly and hold them in trust for those who come after us. We are "temporary possessors and life renters," as Edmund Burke wrote, and we "should not think it amongst [our] rights to commit waste on the inheritance."[1]

Though the commons is everywhere, it is nonetheless little noticed. For economists, it is a kind of inchoate mass that awaits the vivifying hand of the market to attain life. Forests are worthless until they become timber, just as quiet is worthless until it becomes advertising. In this way of seeing things, the enclosure of a commons is always a good thing. Money passes over the commons and says, "Let there be light." The village tree becomes Fox Broadcasting, and trumpets blare in heaven.

So too in politics and the media, where the concept of the commons might as well not exist. There are no news reports on the condition of the commons, no speeches about it in the Senate. Newspapers have many pages of stock market reports but barely a word about wealth that belongs to all of us. Political debate is about the government versus the market. One camp wants to turn everything into something for sale, the other counters with programs of the state. It is a debate between Walmart and welfare, and it leaves no room for anything else.

But of course there is more. The value of the commons is beyond reckoning. Before we can protect it, though, we have to see it, and that is no small task. When we breathe the air or banter with neighbors on the sidewalk, it rarely occurs to us that we are using a commons. A commons has a quality of just being there. People don't need a contract to breathe or an insurance policy to call a neighbor for help. Nor do commons require advertising. The market is always pushing "goods" and "services" in our faces, which might raise doubts as to whether they are really good or really serve. A commons, by contrast, quietly waits to be used.

OF COURSE, SEEING THE COMMONS IS ONLY A FIRST step; the ultimate challenge is to protect it. The solution is not to create new government agencies or programs. Rather, it is to create rules, boundaries, and property rights to protect common wealth, just as we do for private wealth.

This is a crucial point. Societies create private property and societies sustain it. Take away our legal and institutional supports and private property crumbles.

If private wealth requires such an array of props, it is not surprising that common wealth needs as many or more. Private property has lawyers, lobbyists, and bankers on its side. Common wealth, by contrast, is poorly organized, cash short, and inherently nonaggressive. In other words, it needs help.

What forms should such help take? The government should not run a commons any more than it should run businesses, but it can and should set boundaries. For example, it can restrict suburban sprawl through zoning, reserve more of the public airwaves for noncommercial use, and keep the Internet from being taken over by large corporations. Steps like these would not mean more government intrusion into economic, environmental, and social space. Rather, they would make it possible for something besides corporations to occupy these spaces.

Regarding the natural environment, the case is especially strong. The oceans and atmosphere do not belong to government or private corporations. They belong to all of us, and we need institutions that reflect this. One can imagine, for example, trusts that receive polluters' payments and distribute them to all of us as owners. Such institutions would reflect the fact that there are common rights to clean air and water, just as there are private rights to the factories that pollute them. Put commoners in charge of the air, let us charge polluters for using it, and we'll see a lot less pollution than we do now.

2

How Tragic Is the Commons?

In the belief system called economics, it is an article of faith that commons are inherently tragic. Almost by definition, they are tragic because they are prone to overuse. What belongs to all belongs to none, and only private or state ownership can rescue a commons from the sad fate that will otherwise befall it.

The standard reference for this belief is an article that appeared in *Science* in 1968 called "The Tragedy of the Commons."[1] Though the author, Garrett Hardin, was a biologist, his article was strangely lacking in scientific inquiry. It was more like economics—an extrapolation from assumptions rather than an investigation of reality.

Hardin assumed that all commons are free-for-alls. He bid his readers to "picture" a hypothetical pasture peopled with hypothetical herders. These herders existed outside of any social structure and lacked even a capacity to talk with one another. They all behaved according to what the economics texts call "rationality": they let their herds loose in the pasture in a single-minded effort to maximize their own gain, with no thought for the future or for anybody else. Under those assumptions, tragedy is a foregone conclusion.

What Hardin overlooked is that people do not necessarily behave as economists assume they do. As historian E. P. Thompson observed, Hardin failed to grasp "that commoners themselves were not without common sense."[2] Thompson was referring specifically to the common-field agriculture of his own England. Households had their own plots but shared land for hunting, foraging, and grazing. They pooled their implements and labor for joint maintenance and combined their herds to fertilize their respective plots. The destruction Hardin declared to be inevitable simply did not happen. To the contrary, the system worked well for hundreds of years.

The literature is full of similar examples of long-lasting commons. Spain has had shared irrigation systems, called *huerta*, for 600 years. The farmers whose lands adjoin each canal elect their own chief executive, called a *syndic*. They get water from the canal on a rotating basis; during droughts, the crops with the greatest need get first priority. Similarly, in the alpine regions of Switzerland, grazing pastures typically are commons, as are forests, irrigation systems, and the paths and roadways connecting private and common property.

In these places and elsewhere, the commons and the private exist in symbiosis, like the common areas of an apartment co-op or condominium. Each form of property serves the purpose for which it is suited best. Even in the American plains, early cattle ranchers found ways to cooperate rather than destroy the habitat that sustained their herds. They adopted the Mexican practice of branding to distinguish different herds. They cooperated on roundups and cattle drives. And they limited their herds and worked to keep out newcomers. It wasn't always pretty, but it also wasn't the calamity Hardin assumed is unavoidable in open pasture.

Hardin's essay won applause in environmental quarters mainly because it was not really about the commons. It was a case for population control, and the tragedy thesis served as a grim parable to that end. From the start, however, anthropologists and others who actually studied commons objected to Hardin's fabricated thesis; indeed, Elinor Ostrom won a Nobel Prize in economics for explaining the longevity of commons.[3] Eventually, Hardin modified his stance. He acknowledged that overuse is not due to common ownership per se, but to the absence of rules governing access and use.

Overused commons do exist, of course. Fisheries are an example; the atmosphere is another. When overuse occurs, there generally has been a breakdown in the social structures that once governed use, or the scale of breakdown of such structures is difficult to establish.

THE REAL TRAGEDY SURROUNDING THE COMMONS HAS been the invasion by corporate, governmental, and other external forces. Native Americans did not eradicate the buffalo on the western plains; white hunters and soldiers did. Local Appalachians did not slice the tops off mountains; outside corporations did. It is therefore strange that the reigning ideology focuses on the self-destruction of commons when the scale of outside devastation is so much greater.

One reason for the tragedy myth's tenacity may be its implicit remedy: privatization. Privatizing commons usually means corporatizing them. This has its advocates. Unfortunately, when it comes to exploiting the commons, corporations have no built-in capacity to say "enough." They are slaves to quarterly earnings statements and the demands of shareholders, all of which push toward liquidating nature and other commons, not sustaining them.

A paradigmatic example is Pacific Lumber, a California company that in the 1980s owned most of the old-growth redwoods still in private hands. Pacific Lumber was unusual. Its chief executive was a lifelong timberman named A. S. Murphy who believed in harvesting no more than the forests could replace. "Their approach," wrote David Harris in *The Last Stand*, "was to treat the forest as capital and try to live off the interest."[4]

This virtue did not go unpunished. Pacific's self-discipline meant its forests were ripe for less conscientious plucking. Its clean balance sheet—Murphy believed in pay-as-you-go—left plenty of room for a raider to load up the company with debt. And this is exactly what happened.

During the leveraged buyout boom of the 1980s, a corporate chief by the name of Charles Hurwitz teamed up with Michael Milken and Ivan Boesky, two of the more infamous financiers of the era, to take over Pacific Lumber. They mortgaged the company to the hilt to finance the purchase. Then, in order to pay off the debt, Hurwitz began liquidating the forests Murphy had conserved. Finance trumped husbandry, as nowadays it usually does. The result was a tragedy *to*, but not caused *by*, the commons.

3

A New Commons Story

For decades, people have defended the commons and not known it. They've battled pollution, development, corporate marketing assaults on their kids, and so many other things it's hard to keep track. What's been missing is a story that unifies all these seemingly unrelated battles with the force of a powerful idea.

Think about the market story. A few centuries ago, people looked at economic life and saw many seemingly unrelated things. They saw factories and farms, shipping firms and theaters, and so on. Then, in 1776, Adam Smith came along and said, "These aren't separate things. They are different aspects of the same thing—the market."[1] His insight gave mental shape to the whole, and the idea of the market with its beneficent "invisible hand" has dominated public imagination ever since.

It has certainly made life easy for the *Wall Street Journal*. Without the market to cast a devotional glow upon private transactions, the *Journal* would be left with only a welter of deals to report. The market ties those mundane transactions into a larger narrative of uplift and grace. The editorial writers do not have to articulate this, of course; it is embedded in the magical word *market*.

We need to do something similar with the commons—to embed it not with myth but with truth, possibility, and morality. The true part is, The commons is real, huge, and invaluable, and it belongs to all of us. It's also being destroyed—not by itself, but by too much privatization. The possibility part is, We have the capacity to save the commons, though time is short. The moral part is, It's our right and duty to save the commons.

Telling a new commons story won't be easy. Before a new story can take hold, the old one must be contested. That old story goes something like this: Long ago, ordinary people had the right to farm and forage, hunt and fish on property they didn't technically own. People eked out a living but the system was static. No one had an incentive to innovate. Finally, the British Parliament saw the light. Starting in the eighteenth century, it stripped commoners of their rights and made agriculture efficient. The commoners then moved to cities and got jobs in factories. This was the beginning of the modern economy. Today the commons is an interesting relic but of no relevance to the twenty-first century.

This story, of course, is an example of history being written by victors. Native Americans or English peasants before 1700 would have told a different story: the commons served them well before it was taken away. But they lost the property wars and hence the narrative. And there's no lack of contemporary enclosers to keep the old story going. A new commons story must also confront Garrett Hardin's tragedy myth. Hardin's tale was a perfect complement to Adam Smith's. Just as the market according to the latter is inherently creative, so the commons according to the former is inherently self-destructive. Market good, commons bad. It's a formidable one-two punch, except that it isn't true.

IT WAS A GREAT ACHIEVEMENT OF THE ENVIRONMENTAL movement to create a unifying vocabulary. The concerns that came together in the movement existed long before the movement itself. Resource conservation, wilderness preservation, public health, population control, ecology, energy conservation, and anti-pollution regulation were all discussed and practiced to varying degrees, but separately. Most public health workers did not see themselves as part of a movement that included hunters and fishers.

Then Rachel Carson wrote *Silent Spring* and the many became one. They were now aspects of *the environment*, a realm of reality that lies outside the market and that the market isn't automatically entitled to degrade. The word invested the smallest parts with the significance of the whole, much as the term *market* had done for business. Smog no longer was just hazy air; snail darters no longer were just little fish. They now were parts of a larger system in which the health of the whole was bound up with the health of the smallest parts.

Many of us sense that a similar commons story is waiting to be told. In this new story, pollution isn't just a health threat; it's a violation of common rights, a taking of what belongs to all of us. Sprawl isn't just an inefficient use of land and energy; it diminishes the social commons, which withers among freeways and malls. The commercial invasion of childhood is more than a matter of obesity and hyperactivity; it raises the question of who creates the stories on which young people are raised, and to what ends.

The new story of the commons unifies these seemingly unconnected phenomena. It identifies not only the thing aggressed upon—the commons—but also the aggressor—the unconstrained market. It denies that the commons is irrelevant and puts it, properly, at center stage. By so doing it opens the way to a twenty-first-century movement aimed at protecting our shared inheritances and passing them on, undiminished if not enhanced, to our children.

4

A Parallel Economy

For two centuries, economists have regarded the commons as a medieval relic. Money is what really counts, and progress follows in the train of it.

Perhaps this was true for a while. At the start of the industrial age, products were scarce and commons abundant. All the economic gears were arranged to produce more stuff. But times change and scarcities shift. Where once the products of the market were scarce, now it is commons that are scarce, and also most needed. For this reason the commons is not a relic. It is a parallel economy that does real work, a counterpoise to the market that provides antidotes to many pathologies of the modern age.

Take quiet, for example. For centuries, noise has been regarded as a byproduct of progress. Today, Americans rate noise as the number-one urban problem. Not crime or trash, but noise.

Quiet is not a mere amenity. People need it for sleep and concentration, both of which are in short supply. One study showed that kids who live in the rear of apartment buildings do better in school than those who live above noisy streets. The market's answer is drugs for sleeping and concentration—more products for sale, in other words. But does not quiet get better results at less expense? Critics say noise controls are obstacles to the economy. In reality, they are economic measures that meet a real need.

The culture of childhood is another commons that has been invaded. Not long ago, kids played their own games. They were weaned on centuries-old stories that spoke to them at a deep emotional level. Storytelling in families established a bond between generations and provided a window to the adult world. Today this cultural ecosystem is dying. Kids are immersed in narratives constructed for the purpose of making them want things. They play games devised by corporations, and their toys are expensive devices in which the content lies in the product rather than in the child. It is not coincidental that kids are petulant and overweight and have trouble focusing their attention.

Commons-enhancing policies would reestablish boundaries on huckstering to kids—no ads in school, for example. TV shows with embedded ads—called "product placement"—would be clearly labeled so parents can avoid them. The raising of healthy children is no less an economic task than the selling of fattening food and beer. To protect children from commercial predators is not a crimp on the economy; it is a core function of the economy.

If one thing should drive policy toward the commons, it is community. Life was once rich in occasions for spontaneous interaction. People shopped on Main Streets, visited on front porches, attended political events in public venues. Abraham Lincoln and Stephen Douglas had their famous debates in county fairgrounds and town squares all over Illinois, and farmers and townspeople sat for hours in the heat and dust to hear them.

Today most Americans live in suburbs conceived as staging areas for consumption. They move about in the enclosure of cars and shop in the anonymity of malls from which community activities are largely excluded. Politics consists mostly of negative ads shown on television screens. Then people wonder why they feel lonely and depressed, and why the sense of community has vanished.

A better-protected commons would restore opportunities for interaction in daily life. It would encourage cities and suburbs with houses built close together, front porches for visiting, and shops within walking distance. It would encourage mixed uses and granny flats instead of malls and sprawl, and it would build common spaces, such as community gardens, pocket parks, and benches.

Such arrangements are often called the "new urbanism," but actually they are the old village-ism, and they are incubators of friendship and civic engagement. Studies show that the happiest people are those actively involved in helping others. Spatial arrangements that encourage engagement with others can be productive of the happiness people seek.

The market will continue. It answers a genuine need for initiative, enterprise, and yes, products. But the market should exist in equilibrium with a commons economy that does some things better and cheaper. One of government's jobs is to maintain the boundaries between the market and the commons. It should provide a structure of law and support for the commons, just as it does for the market—no more and no less.

5

Stop the Invasions!

To get to San Francisco from where I live, I usually drive through the hamlet of Nicasio. It's just a scattering of wooden structures around a community baseball field. The hills beyond are mainly ranches, not much changed from a century ago.

Recently, a sign appeared by the road there. "SOON TO BE BUILT ON THIS SITE," it said, and my insides went code red. I thought of bulldozers, asphalt, a mange of houses with glandular disorders. Then I saw the smaller print: "Thanks to your help, *absolutely nothing.*"

The sign was the work of a local organization raising funds to buy the land so that developers couldn't. The large type triggered something many Americans feel: a brooding sense of impending loss. This sense begins with wilderness and open space but doesn't end there. Everywhere we look, something we thought was off-limits to the market is falling prey to it: schools, genes, children's imagination and play, urban water systems. Development is decimating our natural ecology just as big box stores are destroying the social ecology of Main Streets.

The environment isn't just about nature anymore. It has become a metaphor for a battle against encroachment that extends to virtually every corner of our society. Everything is up for grabs, everything is for sale. What happened to the common fields of England is happening everywhere.

Water is a prime example. A gift of nature, water has traditionally been available to those who need it, whether through village wells or urban water systems. But today many of these systems are going private. And bottled water has become a huge business, helped by the fact that it's getting hard to find a public water fountain.

Like water, the gene pool has long been a kind of commons. Farmers could draw from it freely, saving seeds from one harvest to use for the next. Now corporations are genetically engineering seeds and obtaining patents on the results. Farmers have to pay royalties when they plant the seeds and can't replant the offspring. They can even be sued for infringement if patented genes are found in their crops, even if they blow over from a neighbor's field.

In the pool of knowledge, so much corporate money is pouring into university labs that research aims increasingly at corporate profit rather than the common good. The University of California at Berkeley dropped its division of biological pest control, in part because corporate funders wanted research on something with more profit potential, such as genetic modifications that can be patented.

In this new setting, the task of defending the commons is bigger and different than it was centuries ago. "In a world where everything is being privatized," wrote Maude Barlow and Tony Clarke in their book *Blue Gold*, "citizens must establish clear perimeters around areas that are sacred to life or necessary for economic and social justice."[1] They were writing about water, but the same can be said of other realms of life that humans have historically shared.

The developed world has turned an economic corner, one that most economists have not grasped. For eons the challenge was to fill the void of material scarcity with the fruits of human ingenuity and toil. That challenge continues in the developing world, but increasingly in the developed world, our challenge is to leave things alone, to let nature and society do the work the market cannot do and, in fact, tends to destroy. In this new, yet old, economy of well-being, the commons plays the central role.

6

The Myopia of Money

Why is the commons invisible? Why does an air conditioner—and the electricity it uses—count in the computations of economic product, but not the cooling provided by shade trees? Why does Disneyland count, but not a local park? Prozac, but not communities that provide human connection and comfort without pharmaceutical products?

The reason, in a word, is money. What is called economics today is the world as seen through the myopic lens of money. If something is transacted through money it has reality; if not, it doesn't exist. It makes no difference that trees provide shade and neighbors provide comfort. Neither is sold for money, and therefore they don't count. As a result, the more our economy displaces that which is free with commodities we have to pay for, the more the economy "grows" and the better life gets, or so we are told.

If you sniff an ideological agenda in this script—well, you are not alone. The mental astigmatism would be comic in a Mr. Magoo way if the implications were not so grim. Our high-level Magoos are engaged in a relentless quest to destroy nonmonetized common wealth in the name of creating monetized private wealth. They count the monetized private gain but not the shared losses, monetized or not, and so believe they are leading us upward when in fact they are taking us into a pit.

When Walmart wipes out a traditional Main Street, economists count the sales at the new superstore but ignore the community—and the social productivity—that were destroyed. When a wetland becomes a shipping channel, they count the new commerce but ignore the lost habitat.

Economists contend that money and price are the truest metrics for what really matters. What they really mean is that money is the only thing they know how to see, and that without this cognitive crutch they are adrift. They cannot pretend to be scientists, do their math, advise presidents, and win Nobels. In fact, a compelling case can be made that the commons often serves authentic needs better and more cheaply than corporate products.

One clue is advertising. Corporations now spend upward of $300 billion a year to cajole us to buy what they sell. Why would they do that if we really needed their stuff?

With commons, such incessant prodding isn't necessary. Central Park does not have to advertise its availability for jogging and picnics. Community gardens have long waiting lists without the help of thirty-second spots. Tap water needs no advertising. People use commons because they are genuinely useful to them, and for that reason alone.

There are other flaws in economists' thinking. To measure value by price, as economists do, assumes an equal ability to pay, which is not the case. If everyone had the same ability to pay, differences in demand for a product would reflect actual differences in the value people attach to it. When incomes are unequal, this is not true. Just because wealthy people spend more on vacations doesn't mean they value vacations more than other people. It simply means they have more money.

Further, the economists' notion of "utility" is one of the great tautologies of all time. You buy something, ergo the thing is assumed to give you "utility." What exactly is the "utility" of a Sara Lee pound cake that was scarfed down by a compulsive eater who then hates herself for doing it? In the end, "utility" is an attempt to cast an aroma of seriousness around the consumption circus.

I'm not suggesting we don't need money or corporate products, but rather that we need the commons too. Yet commons, though they often serve more, remain invisible because their services are literally priceless.

7

Human Nature and the Commons

When Jimmy Wales, a refugee from options trading, set out to create an encyclopedia online, he thought first of the *Britannica* model, except with volunteers. He assigned articles to professional experts and established panels for peer reviews. Then he started to write one himself—on options trading—and realized it was a drag.

It was like "handing in an essay at grad school," he said later. So Wales shifted gears. He kept the volunteer model but made it an open and social experience rather than a hierarchical one. Anyone could write an entry on anything. The peer reviewers would be online readers themselves, who could correct factual errors and omissions and challenge biases.

To a conventional manager it might sound like a recipe for chaos. Yet within two weeks, the project generated more articles than it did in two years of the top-down model. The result is Wikipedia, the free online encyclopedia that now has more than 10 million articles in more than 250 languages.[1]

To an economist it doesn't make sense. People don't work for free. Readers are "consumers," not producers, and consumers don't produce what they consume. Yet they are doing so; and this kind of social coproduction is flourishing not only on the Web but in society at large.

In the United States and elsewhere, people are turning their backs on everyday low prices and choosing the social cohesion of Main Streets instead. Researchers and software designers are foregoing copyrights and patents and releasing their work over the Web for free. In so doing they are enriching the public domain that sustains their work and that of others.

All this defies the supposed "laws" of economics. In terms of the prevailing model, it is as though someone dropped a ball and it went up instead of down. People aren't supposed to work for nothing. They aren't supposed to resist low prices and patent lucre. They aren't supposed to but they do—and not because they are saints but because something in our nature wants to be engaged with other people.

Not long ago it was possible to dismiss such behavior as "alternative." But now it is taking root at the core of the emerging economy. The result has been a kind of Western version of the fall of the Berlin Wall—an enlarged range of economic possibility and a challenge to the central assumptions of economics.

A HUMAN ECONOMY IS A SOCIAL SYSTEM BY DEFINITION. It revolves around relationships and interactions, and the people who actually make the economy work understand this. A copious management literature dwells on such things as teamwork and corporate culture. Advertisers, who must deal with people as they are, play to our cravings for acceptance, belonging, and the like.

It seems so obvious. Yet for most economists, context barely exists. They fixate on a hypothetical molecule of economic action called *homo economicus*. This is the imagined creature who inhabits the economics texts and computer models that are the silent dictators of analysis and policy. He or it seeks only and always to maximize his "utility." He has no social affinities, no lapses of judgment, no capacity for thinking about anyone beside himself. He goes through life with a relentless calculus of personal loss and gain. Basically, he has the emotional development of a three-year-old, only with better math skills.

Homo economicus wasn't born of dispassionate inquiry into human nature, or for that matter, inquiry of any kind. It is a polemical construct designed to achieve particular ends. For the emerging commercial class, greed had to become respectable, the kind of trait a gentleman might cultivate, exercisable without criticism or remorse. Adam Smith's narrative of self-seeking brewers, bakers, and butchers unintentionally promoting a greater good meshed neatly with the aspirations of his day. Later economists, seeking the stature of science, embraced *homo economicus* as a molecule of economic action that was simple and predictable.

Today, psychologists can only roll their eyes at this naïve portrayal. People who deal with actual humans in market settings—such as advertisers and corporate managers—find it borderline irrelevant. Even within the economics profession, a new field called "behavioral economics" is picking *homo economicus* apart. Nevertheless, the model remains the ghost that defines our sense of what is economically possible.

THERE'S ANOTHER SIDE OF HUMAN NATURE THAT LEADS not to markets as the sole realm for economic activity, but to markets and commons in balance. This other side isn't the self-sacrificing altruist that's often posited as the alternative to *homo economicus*. Nor is it the grim utilitarian socialist. Rather, it is the urge within all of us to engage with other people, whether to accomplish a task or just because it is fun.

This convivial side of human nature isn't only what drives a large portion of human activity; it's also a primary source of happiness. Ample research confirms what most of us know from experience: that the happiest people are those most engaged in the lives of others. These studies also show that, beyond a certain threshold of material comfort, more stuff doesn't add much happiness.

We can't flourish without relationships insulated from the demands of money, contracts, and ownership. That's a major reason the commons is so important: it is the economic realm that promotes relationships rather than stuff. And in a multitude of ways, people are trying to resurrect it before the market completely suppresses it.

Consider the World Wide Web, where people connect and share with a minimum of market-imposed restrictions. Social networks facilitate communication among friends. Creative Commons licenses allow creators to distribute music, photos, and other works without legal rigmarole. General Public Licenses keep open source software available to everyone. And of course there's Wikipedia, the largest compendium of human knowledge ever assembled.

Consider also the centers of cities. Portland's Pioneer Square has become a reference point for downtown public spaces, along with older icons such as New York's Central Park and Boston's Common. Recently, Detroit decided to create a large, inviting public space in the middle of the old downtown. The result: people are coming in from the suburbs to experience what the city offers that suburbs can't.

Something similar is happening at the neighborhood level. Instead of retreating to their own patches of urban turf, neighbors are tearing down their back fences to create larger shared spaces. This happened at Montgomery Park, an inner-city oasis in Boston's South End, and it's happening in Baltimore as well. (See chapter 20, "From Alleys to Commons.")

Nowhere is the reclamation of the commons more evident than in regard to food. Food once served as a locus of community, but today that dimension is largely gone. Most of us have no idea where our food comes from, beyond the super-market or the fast-food restaurant. One result has been the social equivalent of empty calories—a hunger that no amount of eating seems to fill.

Farmers' markets have become a way both to improve our diets and our experience of community. The growth in farmers' markets has been remarkable—from 1,755 in the United States in 1994 to more than 7,800 today.[2] Farmers' markets are not only, or even mainly, about organic food. They are about local food and the opportunity to deal directly with the people who produce it. They also are about the festive sociability of the market itself. People go to partake of the bustle and good spirits, something that doesn't much happen at Safeway or even Whole Foods.

Community gardens have grown in a similar manner, and for some of the same reasons. These gardens replicate in urban settings some of the social dynamics of the traditional rural commons. Neighbors share tools and help one another when the need arises.

Ralph Nader's father, a Lebanese immigrant who ran a restaurant in Connecticut, once observed that television "has replaced the dictator's ban on three on more people gathering in one place without a permit." But now that people are reclaiming the urban commons and going out in public again, who knows what will happen?

Cooperation isn't the product solely of individual virtue; much also depends upon the social setting. Whereas commons are, in large part, based on direct encounters between people who know each other, markets are based on transactions among strangers. When a local merchant makes a change mistake in our favor, most of us will point that out. If a credit card company makes such a mistake, we are more likely to think of all the times the company gouged us and consider it rough justice. One tragedy of the market is that it tends to turn us into the kind of people it presumes.

It would be fatuous to suggest that an entire economy could operate on commons principles. The devotees who contribute to Wikipedia and Linux have the time to do so because they get money from the market somehow. The two realms are symbiotic, not mutually exclusive.

What seems clear is that the protected commons needs to be enlarged. It does what the market can't do, and that is what nowadays most needs to be done. We need, increasingly, clean air and convivial communities. We also need markets and the things they produce, but the balance needs to shift.

The movement to resurrect the commons, then, is about more than conserving nature and the equivalents of village trees. Ultimately, it is about resurrecting something in ourselves.

8

Common Property

Property is a mirror; the way we think about it says a lot about the way we think about ourselves. And the way Americans thought about property for much of our history is very different from what most politicians and economists profess today.

In England before America was formed, commoners had rights that were like property rights, even if they weren't called that. Much agricultural land was held in common. In practice this was similar to community gardens today: individuals had their own plots, but the underlying ownership was joint. Pastures for grazing animals were also shared. And no one could keep commoners out of woods and rivers that were open to all. These rights dated back to the Magna Carta, and often before.

The English settlers who came to America carried these traditions with them. Thus, James Madison drafted the Virginia law that made unfenced forests a commons for hunting and fishing. The settlers also embraced what historians call the "civic republican" view of private property. In their minds, private property served an essentially civic purpose. Properly distributed—a crucial proviso—it enabled people to be full citizens. Thomas Jefferson advocated a nation of small farm owners not because he believed in a rural arcadia but because this was the form of property ownership most consistent with civic virtue.

Civic republicanism was also reflected in the corporate charters that prevailed well into the nineteenth century. State legislatures chartered corporations for specific purposes that served a public need, such as building a toll bridge or railroad. Corporations were limited in size and function and their charters expired after a preset number of years.

In the same spirit, early Americans viewed property rights not as a walled fortress but as permeable membranes capable of reconciling parts and the whole. Water law, so important in the new land, reflected this desire for balance. You could use water that ran through your land, but not in a way that diminished your neighbor's use. The Northwest Ordinance of 1787, which laid out a plan for the upper Midwest, declared that the waterways there "shall be common highways and forever free."

Residues of this thinking persist today in the doctrine of the public trust. Roman law declared that some things are common by their very nature—air, wildlife, and navigable waters in particular. Government does not own these and therefore cannot privatize them, even if it wants to. Much like trustees of an estate, governments are legally obliged to maintain these assets for the benefit of all, including future generations.

The trouble with most early common property rights, however, was that they weren't firmly fixed in statutory law. They existed in custom and usage rather than in deeds of ownership. When the British Parliament set out to enclose the commons, no formal property rights stood in its way.

This has been the story of the commons ever since. Whether it is the atmosphere or oceans, the public domain of knowledge or the cognitive environment of our daily lives, it has all been vulnerable to invasion and expropriation because there is no protective legal shell. When a person or corporation takes private property, it is called "theft" and is punished accordingly. When government takes private property, it must, per the Constitution, compensate owners fairly, and it can take private property only for public purposes in the first place. But when a commons is taken it is called "growth," and no punishment or compensation is required.

But can a commons be "propertized"? Would that not make it a carrier of the disease it is supposed to resist? The legal scholar Carol Rose has suggested that a commons can look like property on the outside and support unproperty-like ends on the inside.[1] It all depends on how the property rights are structured.

Property is not a metaphysical absolute. It is a construct, a bundle of rights that changes with the context. A first-year law student learns this early on. Partnership rights are different from shareholder rights. Rights in a cooperative are different from those in a condominium. Property in a marriage is different from that in a mutual fund. They are all property, but they are encoded differently to achieve different ends.

To give a commons legal status as property is to give it a protective shell; corporations and governments then can't trespass or take it. The question is, What kind of shell is most appropriate for a commons?

In some cases government ownership can work, as with libraries and parks. But state ownership is always subject to power and policy shifts, and privatization is never off the table.

In many cases the legal structure of not-for-profit trusts can be applied to commons. People establish trusts for the benefit of future generations. In the case of family trusts it's the children or grandchildren. Nonfamily trusts exist for forests, community-owned land, universities, and many other things. In all cases, trustees have a fiduciary duty to manage the trust's assets for the sole benefit of the designated beneficiaries.

However the outer shell is constructed, common property can be encoded internally to counterbalance the tendencies of private property. Where corporate property is encoded to benefit the few (shareholders), common property can be encoded to benefit the many. And just as corporate property is managed for short-term gain, so common property can be managed for the long haul. These imperatives need not be imposed by government regulatory agencies. Rather, they can be embedded in the property itself and enforced like all property rights through the courts.

9

Takers and Givers

The "takings theory" beloved by conservatives says that every government restriction on the use of private property represents a "taking" in violation of the Fifth Amendment, and that taxpayers must compensate affected property owners accordingly.

A typical expression of this theory comes from Janice Rogers Brown, a justice on the California Supreme Court. Brown says that zoning laws are a form of "theft," which means they require compensation from the rest of us.[1] If zoning laws prevent property owners from, say, building a gas station or convenience store on their lot, then according to this view they should be able to demand compensation from their neighbors for "damages."

And it's not just zoning laws. Brown would reverse Supreme Court decisions that upheld bans on sweatshops, child labor, and workplace hazards, because they represent takings from the businesses involved.

Brown and her cohorts are not reticent about their aims. Richard Epstein, a University of Chicago law professor and leading proponent of the takings theory, says he wants to "invalidate much of the twentieth century legislation."[2]

What these thinkers forget is that a lot of what people say is "theirs" came as gifts from the rest of us. Land is a prime example. The value of a parcel in downtown Manhattan has little to do with the owner's efforts (we are talking about the land here, not the structures on it) and much to do with society as a whole. It results from the investments of surrounding property owners and of the city, the latter in the form of streets, parks, sanitation, transportation, and so on.

The same could be said of just about all property. In my work I use the World Wide Web, a social creation that accounts for much of the value of my computer. And where would oil companies be without our massive infrastructure for automobiles, not to mention our military presence in the Middle East? For that matter, where would any corporation or investor be without a functioning stock market, which is a social creation rather than the work of those who benefit from it?

Commons thinking makes it clear that those who claim an absolute right to do anything with their property are often recipients of vast "givings." Consider New Orleans. Hurricanes and floods are not exactly new to that city. No sooner had the first settlement been built in 1723 than a fierce hurricane wiped it out. Eventually, the city built an elaborate system of pumps and levees to keep floods and storms at bay. Every property owner in New Orleans is thus dependent upon massive public spending, without which private holdings would be worthless.

In less dramatic ways, all wealth is in fact a coproduction among an owner, society, and nature. In many cases, the bulk of the value comes from the latter two. The levees that surround New Orleans in a sense surround us all. The problem is that some want to pretend they keep the water away by their own enterprise and virtue.

For almost every "taking" there is a giving, and often a great many of them. We the givers are the silent majority, and it is time for us to stand up for our rights.

10

The Community of Goods

We reveal ourselves in our instinctive response to another's need. When, during Hurricane Katrina, authorities saw people breaking into stores in New Orleans, they saw it as a threat to property rather than a desperate need for food and water. In truth, of course, both were involved, but there is a legal tradition that justifies the taking of food in such circumstances, and it comes from the natural law teachings so favored by rightward judges. It is called the doctrine of "overruling necessity," and it says that property is secondary in times of urgent human need.

The property claims of the rich man "must give way to the pressing and preferable Title of those who are in danger to perish without it," wrote John Locke in his *Second Treatise on Government* (1690). "Necessity sets property aside," wrote Thomas Rutherford, a noted eighteenth-century legal commentator, in his *Institutes of Natural Law* (1754). At such times there is a "community of goods."

This thinking found expression in the doctrine that sailors in distress could find hospitality in British ports whatever their nation of origin. It authorized communities to tear down buildings deemed fire hazards without compensating owners. It allowed people to hunt and fish on other peoples' land so long as it wasn't fenced. When push came to shove, the need for sustenance trumped rights of private property.

What is most interesting, though, is how the proponents of "the community of goods" justified it. It was not that a needy individual had a claim on what belonged to other people. Rather, it was that the needy person had a prior property right—a common property right—that superseded private property in this circumstance.

At some point in the past, the argument went, all property was held in common. From this common pool, individuals asserted private claims, justified by their toil upon the land. But these private claims are provisional, not absolute. They are valid in normal times, but not all times. "In cases of extreme necessity," observed Hugo Grotius, the seventeenth-century jurist, "the original right of using things, as if they had remained in common, must be revived; because in all human laws, and consequently all laws relating to property, the case of extreme necessity forms an exception."

Natural law theory assumes that people consent to the impositions of society through an implied contract. Property is part of that contract. "No one," observes historian William Novak, summarizing the commentators, "could be assumed to have consented away the right to use another's property when self or social preservation were in jeopardy."[1]

None of this justifies wanton looting. A society cannot function with jungle law, at the bottom or the top. But it does make us question our current arrangements for using the nation's vast wealth for meeting urgent human needs. If a revival of the law of overruling necessity arises from the destruction of Katrina, that would be a good thing.

Conservative Commoners,
Once

Few things would shake up American politics as much as clarifying the term *conservative*. From the daily media one might surmise that conservatives are people who hate taxes and gays and love markets and religion. But the conservative tradition runs deeper than that, and in some ways contrary to it.

Conservatism is, or at least used to be, a way of thinking about society as a whole and the qualities that help maintain it. Edmund Burke, the father of Anglo-Saxon conservatism, believed society is an organic whole—a "community of souls," as his twentieth-century follower Russell Kirk put it.[1]

This view of society has large implications. For one thing, it means that people have a duty to support the whole with taxes. "Are all the taxes to be voted grievances?" Burke asked rhetorically, and dismissively, in his *Reflections on the Revolution in France* (1790). For another, it means that humanity must take the long view. Society is a partnership "not only between those who are living," Burke wrote, "but between those who are living, those who are dead, and those who are to be born." It is true that private property played a central role in the original conservative view. But this was individual, not corporate property, and it was embedded in the same web of mutual obligation that individuals themselves were.

As corporations became dominant in modern life, some writers in the Burkean tradition saw a threat to conservative values. One was Kirk, an intellectual godfather of the modern conservative movement. His book, *The Conservative Mind*, bristles with concern about commercial culture. It cites with approval Coleridge's view that the source of England's problems was the "overbalance of the commercial spirit in consequence of the absence or weakness of counterweights."[2]

Kirk was in some ways a fusty aristocrat, but he was honest enough to acknowledge as a conservative that markets need boundaries, just as the state does. Others were equally explicit. Wilhelm Ropke, for example, an Austrian economist greatly influenced by Ludwig von Mises, wrote a book called *A Humane Economy* in which he reflected on the limits of the market he had championed all his life.[3] "The highest interests of the community and the indispensable things of life have no exchange value and are neglected if supply and demand are allowed to dominate the field," he wrote. "The supporters of the market economy do it the worst service by not observing its limits and conditions." This is not a liberal talking (except in the classical sense). It is a conservative who, according to the Ludwig von Mises Institute, "devoted his career to combating collectivism in economic, social and political theory."[4]

In recent decades authentic conservatism—the kind that respects community, locality, tradition, and virtue—has been displaced by a phony kind that is politically expedient and cynical to the core. It channels the conservative impulse into a few red-meat issues—abortion, gays, school prayer—that pose no threat to the bankrollers of either party. Thus, one does not often hear a Fox News commentator talk about the limits of the market, as opposed to what else should be given over to it. What this phony "movement" really professes is not conservatism but the opposite—a belief that it is okay to waste the patrimony so long as somebody makes money doing it. Edmund Burke would be turning in his tomb.

PRACTICE

Jonathan Rowe wasn't only a thinker; he was also a doer and an admirer of doers. In this part of the book he discusses current and potential efforts to make the commons a vibrant counterweight to the market.

One new practice he invites is better accounting of common wealth. This would reveal that much of what we think is growth is in fact a cannibalization of assets we depend on. No business would last long if it were managed this way.

Other practices Rowe wants more of would enlarge the public domains of science, art, and ideas. The Constitution allows patents and copyrights for "limited times" only because, in the founders' minds, the purpose of these monopolies is to populate the world of freely exchanged ideas. Today, long-lasting intellectual property rights impede creativity and research.

Rowe envisioned other practical twenty-first-century uses of the commons. For example, time-banking systems could match unmet human needs with people willing and able to meet them. And trusts that charge market prices for use of common resources could generate cash income for millions. A proven model for this is the Alaska Permanent Fund, which pays all Alaskans equal dividends from state oil leases. "This isn't wealth redistribution," Rowe observes "It is a return to owners for use of their property."

Chapter 15, "Build It and They Will Sit," tells how Rowe and a friend seeded a commons in their home town. They fixed up some old garden benches, deposited them in a vacant lot, added a bunch of tree stumps, and waited. Very quickly, an informal town square took shape.

Other practical measures Rowe encourages include municipal wi-fi, open source software, farmers' markets, trusts to protect ecosystems, and more time off from jobs. He concludes that seeds of a new commons movement are spreading. What are needed now, he says, are new commons institutions and property rights, and "government nurturing the commons as zealously as it nurtures corporations."

— *Ed.*

Accounting for
Common Wealth

Amerina's economic accounting is a lot like Enron's before
the dam broke. There are missing ledger pages that would
show a hemorrhaging of debt, and a special entry called "externalities" into which hidden obligations are stashed.

Virtually all forms of accounting today overlook these liabilities, and a trove of hidden assets too. A report called *The
State of The Commons* evaluates the current management of
America's common wealth and finds that maintenance is ter-
rible, theft is rampant, and rents often aren't being collected.
In other words, our common wealth—and our children's—is
being squandered, and we all are poorer as a result.[1]

Consider, for example, water. All told, America is taking
75 gallons of groundwater for every 60 that nature puts back
in. The Ogallala Aquifer, which stretches from North Dakota
to Texas and supports a fifth of the irrigated farmland in the
United States, is half gone. In 2001, the Rio Grande ceased to
flow into the Gulf of Mexico.

No business would last long if it managed its balance sheet like that. Enron didn't. Yet, because there's no accounting for the water commons, Americans don't get the message. It takes more than 100,000 gallons of water to make one automobile, but automakers don't pay for damaged water tables. What looks like growth is really depletion in disguise.

So too with the Earth's atmosphere, a prolific source of value that protects us from ultraviolet rays, keeps temperatures stable, delivers oxygen, and replenishes fresh water. No human-made product comes close in terms of usefulness. Yet corporations have been using the atmosphere as an unlimited waste dump, and the damages consequently accrued are both enormous and ignored.

Thus, carbon dioxide levels are up dramatically since the beginning of the industrial age, and as a result, temperatures are rising, polar ice is melting, and extreme weather events like droughts, heat waves, and hurricanes are more frequent and stronger. According to Munich Re, a global reinsurance company, the economic cost of weather-related disasters has exceeded $1 trillion since 1980 and is showing "a significant long-term upward trend."[2]

Water and air are just two of many examples. The point is that when the market expands, it doesn't do so into a void. Often, it displaces or disturbs something that is already there—a commons—that serves real needs. If we aren't careful, the market will destroy its own golden goose. This is bound to happen if we don't account for the commons and connect that accounting to institutional and individual behavior.

If Enron taught us anything, it is that reality prevails sooner or later. Our choice is to count our common wealth or pretend it doesn't exist. If our grandchildren could be consulted, we know which path they'd have us choose.

Tollbooths of the Mind

I f one thing is central to the idea of America, it is the ability to breathe freely in the atmosphere of the mind. Thomas Jefferson was the champion of this idea, and he saw that government was not the only threat to it.

"If nature has made any one thing less susceptible than all others of exclusive property," Jefferson wrote, "it is the action of the thinking power called an idea."[1] Share money and you have less; share an idea and you still have it, and more.

Benjamin Franklin expressed a similar view when he explained why he didn't seek patents on his numerous inventions. "As we enjoy great advantages from the inventions of others," he wrote, "we should be glad to serve others by any invention of ours."[2]

In this spirit, the Constitution restricted government-bestowed intellectual monopolies—patents and copyrights—to "limited times," after which writings and inventions would flow back into the public domain that nurtured them. Jefferson practiced what he preached, in this respect at least. Like

Franklin, he refused to patent his own inventions because he believed invention to be the property of humankind. As the nation's first commissioner of patents, he did not grant these monopolies easily. His aim was to enrich the public domain, not the private monopolizers of ideas.

This vision prevailed in America for two centuries, more or less. The result was more enterprise, research, and invention than the world had ever seen. To be sure, our nation had its share of patent hounds, Thomas Edison not least of them. But in the realm of science, the Jeffersonian ethos prevailed. Jonas Salk, who discovered the first polio vaccine, was once asked who would own the new drug. "There is no patent," Salk replied. "Could you patent the sun?"[3]

Today, that question would not be rhetorical. Fences and tollgates are rising rapidly on the commons of the mind. Copyright and patent monopolies have gone far beyond what the founders intended. Corporations now claim ownership of everything under the sun, if not the sun itself: body parts, business practices, DNA. They even claim ownership of the English language. McDonald's has asserted trademark claims to 131 common words and phrases, such as "Always Fun" and "Made For You."[4]

Supposedly, this ownership frenzy serves as an incentive for invention and discovery. But more often the opposite is the case. In university labs, secrecy and paranoia have replaced collegiality. Researchers now must navigate a minefield of competing patent claims. A new virus-resistant strain of rice can't be sold because it needs approvals from so many different patent holders. At MIT some graduate students don't want to defend their theses for fear of revealing proprietary information.

As for copyrights, the original term was fourteen years. Now, it is the lifetime of the creator plus seventy years. If this expansion has brought a corresponding improvement in literary quality, it is not apparent from the bestseller lists. But it's a huge profit booster for companies like Disney and Microsoft, who pay us nothing for it.

Another place fences are going up is on the World Wide Web. The Internet began much like America itself, as a commons open to all. The idea, observes law professor Lawrence Lessig, was "never to allow anyone to decide what would be allowed."[5] Then corporations moved in. Websites became loaded with commercials, and search engines turned into payola stations. Now some companies are pushing for a two-tier Internet in which their content gets preference over others'.

There is resistance to these trends, of course. Yet inch by inch, Jefferson's vision for America is turning upside down. Centuries ago the concept of private property emerged as a means of liberation. It helped break the shackles of royal power and served as a bulwark against the state. But as Jefferson intuited, taken too far, private property becomes another version of what it once opposed.

The challenge now is to restore the balance between the private and the common that the founders sought to establish.

"If communism versus capitalism was the struggle of the 20th century," Lessig writes, "then control versus freedom will be the debate of the 21st."[6]

14

Subsistence from the Commons

Southern planters faced a major dilemma after the Civil War. Not only had they lost their slaves; now many former slaves refused to work on the terms the planters offered. The freedmen had become too independent, it was said, and a big part of that newfound independence involved access to the commons.

In the American South, the commons took the form of law and custom allowing people to hunt, fish, and even graze cattle on land they did not own, as long as the owner put no fence around it. Private property rights yielded to the needs of subsistence—to common rights. In this way the commons supported blacks during their long bondage and after emancipation gave them a measure of economic independence. Which is why, of course, it had to go.

Across the South in those years, planters did what their counterparts in England had done before: they closed the commons and declared private land off-limits, fenced or not, regardless of whether the owner put it to use. In England, the enclosures drove commoners into the cities, where they supplied a desperate labor force for the mills. In the American South, the effect was to help force former slaves back into submission as sharecroppers or low-wage help. "Believing black dependency to be the handmaiden of work discipline," Steven Hahn observed in *The Roots of Southern Populism*, "the planters moved to circumscribe the freedmen's mobility and access to the means of production and subsistence."[1]

Nowadays we associate the means of production and subsistence with the market, but that sets the frame too narrowly. From the moment the Pilgrims landed on Cape Cod, the commons was central to America's material sufficiency. (For Native Americans, of course, it was almost the entire source of material sufficiency.) The first European settlers built towns around a shared pasture for livestock, which they actually called a commons. In North and South alike, private woodlands were open for hunting or wood-cutting unless owners fenced them. A Massachusetts ordinance of 1641 declared that "any man . . . may pass on foot through any man's property" to fish or fowl at common ponds.

Today the privatization of common wealth has reached historic heights, and it is not coincidental that, as these takings have accelerated, so has the gap between the rich and everyone else. But it is not too late to ask whether the commons again can be a source of subsistence for many.

TO RESURRECT THE COMMONS AS A TWENTY-FIRST-CENTURY source of subsistence, it helps to start with things that are part of daily life. Like fishing. Some 35 million Americans fish, and a fair number of them live in cities. A visit to Hains Point on the Potomac River in Washington, D.C., or to the Oakland waterfront in California, would illustrate the point. Most cities are built on water and would be good fishing sites if the water were not so foul.

Or consider community gardens, small urban farms on land the gardeners themselves do not own. There are now some 18,000 such gardens in the United States, according to the American Community Gardening Association. That name might call to mind urban dilettantes with Smith and Hawken hoes; in fact, community gardens represent real production meeting real needs. The Food Project in Boston raises 120,000 pounds of fresh vegetables on 21 acres; most of that goes to people who need it. In Philadelphia, urban gardeners (by their own reckoning) save some $700 a year on food bills.

But the needs of far more people could be served. There are some 70,000 parcels of vacant land in Chicago and 1,000 in Philadelphia; vacant lots occupy 18 percent of Trenton, New Jersey. This land could become a prolific urban commons that helps ordinary people subsist. In 1943, in the midst of World War II, Americans raised half our supply of fresh vegetables in Victory Gardens, as they were then known. We could do as well today.

A MODERN ECONOMY, HOWEVER, IS MOSTLY A MONETARY economy. It is therefore appropriate to think of the commons as a source not just of food but also of money to meet subsistence needs. If the commons belongs to all of us, then financial returns from the commons should flow to all of us as well. To be sure, commons should stay free when more use enhances the whole. For example, when more people use the Internet, it becomes more valuable and should therefore remain freely open. Many commons, however, are diminished by excessive use. In those cases, when one person takes, others become poorer. Extract minerals from public lands and there's less left for future generations. Use the air as a waste dump and others breathe less freely. When these commons are diminished, the diminishers should pay the owners—which is to say, all of us.

A prototype for this sort of compensation is the Alaska Permanent Fund, which since 1976 has distributed income from state oil leases equally to all Alaskans. Each year, every adult and child in the state receives a dividend of around $1,500. This isn't wealth redistribution; it is a return to owners for use of their property. Because the property in question is common, it is also a modern commons contributing to its members' subsistence.

A similar model has been proposed as an antidote to climate change—a "sky trust" that charges dumpers of carbon into our atmosphere and returns the proceeds to all Americans equally. A bill cosponsored by Senators Maria Cantwell of Washington and Susan Collins of Maine would set up such a system. Conveniently, the higher the pollution charges, the higher the dividends. Less climate change and greater individual income would go together.

It's possible to apply the same principle to other limited commons: parking space, rush-hour driving lanes, the airwaves, minerals and timber on public lands. At the moment, however, we mostly do the opposite. American taxpayers spend more on roads for private timber companies operating on public land than we get back in fees for the timber they cut there. Thanks to the still-regnant Mining Law of 1872, removers of minerals from public land pay a pittance for the profitable privilege. And media companies pay nothing at all for the right to flood our airwaves with ads. All these sweetheart deals represent a massive squandering of common wealth. If broadcasters paid to use our airwaves, that alone would earn us billions of dollars a year.

In the same way, commoners could also collect royalties for the patent monopolies we currently grant to private corporations for free. The case for such royalties is especially compelling when we, as taxpayers, fund the research that leads to a patent, as often happens in the pharmaceutical sector.

BEHIND THE CONCEPT OF PRICING THE COMMONS LIES a deeper vision of where wealth comes from. Virtually all "private" wealth emerges from collaboration among individuals, society, and nature. The most "self-made" men and women draw upon a vast pool of knowledge and natural gifts they did nothing to create. They also benefit from schools, roads, and other public services, including enforcement of contracts and property rights. Warren Buffett, whose candor is in the same league as his wealth, says that society is responsible for "a very significant percentage of what I've earned."

If private wealth is partly common wealth, there are monetary implications. One is that takers should pay for what they take, and those payments should go to all of us collectively or in equal shares. Another is that taxation should distinguish between wealth created and wealth taken from the commons. The former should be lightly taxed and the latter heavily.

This latter principle isn't new; it informed the original income tax of 1913, which applied only to large "unearned" gains. Representative Dan V. Stephens of Nebraska spoke for many when he said that the new revenues should come from the "surplus wealth of the nation that has already been collected into private hands in abnormal proportions." The income of ordinary working Americans was not taxed at all until World War II.

If we structured taxes this way—if we taxed earned wealth lightly and taken wealth heavily—taxes would seem less an imposition and more an outgrowth of moral and economic principles. In the economy itself, taxes wouldn't impede genuine wealth creation but rather would encourage it. Of course, this is the exact opposite of what we do now.

We can't go back to the days when woods and streams sustained daily life. But we can go back to the principles that made those commons sustaining and fruitfully apply them to our economy today.

15

Build It and They Will Sit

William H. Whyte was a journalist who spent years observing how people act and interact in public spaces. He walked the streets, sat with notebook in plazas and parks, set up cameras in unobtrusive places, and spent endless hours studying the results. He noticed that when people stop to chat on sidewalks they don't move to an edge or entryway, they stay right in the middle. Others have to walk around them. In plazas they tend to congregate where other people are. Even lovers don't seek the solitude of secluded corners, as one might expect. They coo right out in the open, for all to see.

"It is difficult to design a space that will not attract people," Whyte wrote. "What attracts people most is other people." And yet, remarkably, many cities have succeeded in designing "under-crowded" public spaces, sometimes very grand and beautiful ones. The reason, Whyte found, is that people don't care about the architectural design of a public space. What they care about is one simple thing: places to sit. They especially like steps and ledges, perhaps because they don't appear intended for sitting. And they like chairs they can move around, so they can create their own groups or sit apart and read.[1]

Which brings me to a vacant—that is, undeveloped—lot on Main Street in my town, right next to a gift shop and a bakery. The bakery has a couple of benches outside, and in the mornings the place is buzzing. More than one person has noted that the adjacent vacant lot would make a natural extension of it. There could be more benches, some tables for eating or for chess, maybe a play area for little kids. It could be the heart of town.

A friend and I decided to see if we could make a commons happen there just by seeding it a bit. We both had old garden benches lying around, so we fixed them up and painted them. Then we deposited them without ceremony on the lot, added a bunch of tree stumps, and waited.

Without any marketing or hype, people quickly started using the benches, talking and sipping or just resting their feet. Lo and behold, this ad hoc commons produced not a tragedy but rather a comedy in the root sense of that word.

I was hoping for something like that. What I didn't anticipate was how good I'd feel. The people sitting there don't know where the benches came from, but I do. My son, who helped me paint them, feels great pride as well. Part of the hidden narrative of a commons is the rewards it gives to those who make it better.

What makes this "commons" possible is that the private owner of the lot is an older man who lives about 20 miles away and for whatever reason has been happy to let the lot sit empty. Lately we heard that the owner has gone into a home, which raises concerns about the heirs. Will the property fall to the son or daughter with an MBA who will look at the family inventory and see—horrors!—an underperforming asset? Will the lot be sold to conform to the strict code of economically correct behavior, or to appease a petulant sibling? We are discussing contingency plans. But meanwhile it is clear that the threat to our commons is not the inherent "tragedy" of it, but rather the tragedy that might arise from profit-maximizing ownership of it.

EDITOR'S NOTE: *The vacant lot on Main Street in Point Reyes Station has now been formally leased by West Marin Commons. It has become the de facto town commons and is informally known as Jon Rowe Park.*

16

Sidewalks of the
Information Age

My mother's second husband grew up on a farm in Texas. He was not liberal. He railed about men who spent the winter on unemployment, and he thought criminals had it coming, the worse the better. Yet he also revered Franklin Delano Roosevelt (FDR).

Partly it was the farm programs that rescued many from the depths, but mainly it was public power. In Texas, as in most of the country, private utilities had bypassed rural areas because they weren't worth serving, in the utilities' view at least. Too much cost, not enough profit. Yet the utilities jealously guarded their monopolies and resisted efforts of legislators to serve those in need.

Finally, FDR pushed through the Rural Electrification Act. Cooperatively owned utility poles went up along dirt roads. Wires went from the utility poles to farmhouses. One momentous day, light bulbs went on in farm kitchens and refrigerators began to purr. It was like the Red Sea parting. My stepfather's evocation of the taste of cold milk in the brutal Texas heat is something I will never forget. Texas was Democratic for as long as that memory survived.

BROADBAND INTERNET ACCESS ISN'T ELECTRICITY, BUT it's pretty important nonetheless. The business of daily life is moving increasingly online, and those who aren't there will slip out of the game. People not served by broadband are in something of the position of those who weren't served by electricity several generations ago.

The comparison is especially fitting with regard to the providers—or more precisely, the nonproviders—of these services. Broadband companies are bypassing poor families today the way the private utilities bypassed farms long ago. In Philadelphia fewer than 25 percent of low income families are connected to the Internet.[1] Cost is the main reason, surveys say.

This is one reason Philadelphia is establishing municipal wi-fi networks to make sure everyone gets served. These networks also will help local businesses and increase efficiency for local governments.

Cable and telecoms companies have mounted a furious counterattack, and legislatures in thirteen states have imposed restrictions or outright bans on municipal wi-fi. That includes Pennsylvania, though the legislature exempted Philadelphia from the ban because its system was so far along.

The main argument of the Internet providers is that the cities are trying to socialize a function that ought to be left to private enterprise. This argument is bogus but points to a useful question: What functions are best served by private companies, and what are better provided by a commons in one form or another?

Consider sidewalks, one of the greatest human inventions. At any given hour, people use them to shop, gawk, play ball, or meet the object of their affections. All this for a minimal amount of upkeep and expense.

It would have been possible, I suppose, to privatize sidewalks, erect tollbooths at every block, and build walls so people couldn't sneak through someone's yard. It would have been possible, but our cities and lives would not have been better for it.

Commons are a form of social lubrication. Some things must be free or cheap for the rest of life—including markets—to function smoothly. Free sidewalks bring customers to the merchant's door. Free information feeds invention that becomes new enterprise. The commons feeds the market and the market feeds the commons. Pure symbiosis.

Broadband access is now the sidewalk of the information age. It is a means of connection—a way to transact whatever business or pleasure the user has in mind. If a city can provide concrete sidewalks, why can't it provide electronic ones? What's the hang-up here?

Municipal wi-fi isn't a step toward socialism any more than free sidewalks are. Free sidewalks mean more business, not less, for enterprises that connect to them. Just so, city-provided wi-fi is good for enterprises that do business via the Web, as opposed to those that sell connections. The argument that municipal wi-fi is bad for free enterprise is totally specious. The issue here is corporate self-interest, not moral principle.

When FDR's co-ops extended wires to isolated farms, private enterprise did not suffer. To the contrary, it had new customers for light bulbs and refrigerators and many other things. Even markets benefit from a world in which some things aren't run for private profit.

Reallocating Time

No man is an island, the poet John Donne wrote, and neither is the market. It needs a realm outside itself— a commons—for sustenance and life. It needs a *natural* commons in the form of water, air, trees, and the like. It needs a *social* commons in the form of language, sidewalks, community and respect for law. And it needs a *temporal* commons, a pool of time available for work outside the market. If this extra-market work doesn't get done—if no one cares for young and old, serves as neighbor and friend, or attends to the work of the community—then the market itself will eventually collapse.

There is thus a symbiosis, and also a competition, between the market and the commons for our finite time as living beings. In recent decades, however, the distribution between the two sectors has gotten seriously out of whack. The market has been claiming more and more of our time, just as it has been claiming more of nature. Never before in history has a society expended so much time on monetarily enriching work—trading derivatives, for example—while neglecting so much work that really needs to get done.

"For the first two-thirds of the twentieth century," writes sociologist Robert Putnam in his book *Bowling Alone*, "a powerful tide bore Americans into ever deeper engagement in the life of their communities, but a few decades ago—silently, without warning—that tide reversed and we were overtaken by a treacherous rip current. Without at first noticing, we have been pulled apart from one another and from our communities."[1]

Putnam's thesis provoked controversy when he first published it in the mid-1990s. But for most Americans, it confirmed a gnawing sense of deficit and loss. A decade ago, the Ford Foundation found that the United States had a deficit of some one million volunteers in child care alone, and the situation has worsened since then.

What's been gobbling up our time? Partly it's the longer hours we have to work to pay our bills, but that's not the whole story. We're also spending more time getting to and from work. And thanks to e-mail and cell phones, we're also working when we're not physically "at work."

During the late 1990s, a scene became familiar in the coffee shops of the city where I lived. A family of tourists would be sitting at a table. Mom would be nursing her coffee. The kids would be picking at their muffins, feet dangling in the air. The mood would be desultory, even a bit sullen. Meanwhile, Dad would be pushing back from the table, talking business into a cell phone. He was physically present but not really there.

There are other ways the workplace has expanded. For example, businesses have turned their customers—us—into unpaid workers. Where not long ago businesses had telephone operators to direct our calls, we now navigate labyrinthine answering systems, step by exasperating step, and often several times over. The company saves on labor, but our time is wasted.

On top of that is the time we spend dealing with the deluge of decisions the market brings daily to our door. Economists hail the deregulation of telephone service, banking, and energy for increasing the "choices" we enjoy. But choices involve a hidden cost in the form of time. Those hours we spend puzzling over the options of medical insurance, cell phone and investment plans, and then dealing with disputes over bills, are hours not available for other pursuits. And thanks to the Internet, our time for struggling with market choices can fill virtually every waking moment.

IN THE AMERICAN WEST, THERE IS A GROWING MOVE-ment to tear down dams so that water can flow back to its most beneficial uses. In much the same way, there's a need to release time back into the commons.

To put it another way, more flexibility to the workday, and more time off, does not mean a slackening of work effort.

Rather, it means a shifting of work time from the market to the commons. The best thing Bill Clinton did as president may have been the Family and Medical Leave Act, which enabled parents to spend up to four months with newborn children before returning to work. Business lobbyists predicted economic disaster. Instead, we had an economic boom, and parents got a few months to be real parents.

There is a need for more enclaves of time like that. Time not consumed by the market is not necessarily time lost to lethargy and waste. When we are not working or shopping, we are often doing genuinely useful things. We might be working on a project with our kids or attending a town meeting. Or we might be sitting on a front porch, providing watchful eyes that help keep a neighborhood safe.

We need to protect our time as well as our waters and wilderness. We also need ways to channel nonmarket time into constructive uses. One such channel is the time-banking system described in the next chapter.

Time is the basic human resource and the starting point of freedom. To use more time for commons work could be the next freedom movement, the one that truly claims the promise of the Industrial Revolution.

18

Time Banking

A basic function of a society is to bring needs and resources together. But in America today, vast needs exist alongside vast resources of unused time, particularly among retired people and the young.

The first impulse might be to call this a failure of markets, since the market is how Americans believe needs and resources come together. But the failure here is on the commons side—a failure of the informal safety net upon which society depends. Grandpa used to move in with Aunt Millie or one of the kids. Of course, this system hardly worked for everyone, which is why we needed Social Security. But families and neighbors did provide a lot of care for those who could not provide for themselves.

One ingenious model for repairing the social safety net was developed by Elderplan, a health maintenance organization (HMO) for seniors in Brooklyn. Elderplan began as one of several so-called "social" HMOs funded by Congress in 1985. The original idea was to tack social services onto the HMO model, thereby preventing medical problems and reducing costs. (Old people often stay in hospitals much longer than necessary because they have no care at home.) But Elderplan soon ran up against the familiar wall. Social services cost money too, and there just wasn't enough money to meet the need.

So Elderplan enlisted its members in taking care of one another. No cash is involved. For each hour members spend helping one another, they get a credit in a computer system that they can draw on when they need help themselves. The tracking units are called "Time Dollars."

Herbie Fine is an Elderplan member who took hold of the new system with a passion. A widower and retired movie and film developer in his mid-seventies, Fine devoted much time to caring for other members in their nineties. He would take them to hospital emergency rooms in the middle of the night, do the shopping, call or visit almost every day. He called these partners *boychiks*, a Yiddish word of affection. Then Herbie fell ill and was confined to his apartment. Elderplan members came to visit every day and made sure his needs were met. "What is Elderplan?" Herbie says. "It's helping one another out. Like a family." Not many Americans would describe their insurance companies in such terms.

There are thousands of Herbie Fines today involved in networks like this throughout the country. In the barrio of El Paso, impoverished Mexican immigrants are paying for medical care at a local clinic by helping in public health projects and providing rides to the clinic. In the old Cuban neighborhood of Miami, retirees are staffing a day care center for working mothers, gaining credits they can use to obtain help from the parents on weekends. Increasingly, these programs are expanding to build bonds between generations. In Washington, D.C., for example, high schoolers are doing yard work for seniors; the students then donate their credits to other seniors in need.

Historically, people have often resorted to barter in times of need. During the Depression, a few men living in a sewer pipe in Oakland started a system called the Unemployed Exchange Association (UXA) that grew into a statewide barter network involving more than 100,000 members. But such networks generally decline when the money economy revives. The New Deal and cash-paying jobs provided by the Works Progress Administration brought the UXA down.

Time banking is different because it is not a substitute for the market economy. Rather, it replicates the social bonds that once flourished in the nonmarket economy by functioning as the memory bank in which good deeds are recorded and potentially returned.

At the most practical level, the time bank multiplies the care that Elderplan can provide. Human liabilities become productive assets when freed from the market's money-driven way of doing things. The time bank also cuts costs by enabling members to stay at home instead of nursing homes. And it gives seniors something the market generally denies them: a sense that they are useful and needed. "When you give to someone, you get so much in return," says Ray Hughes, a retired merchant seaman in the program. "You want to keep going."

Critics of time banks say they violate the spirit of volunteerism by giving a reward for deeds that ought to be done for free. But what's wrong with a system in which good deeds are returned? Wasn't that the premise behind barn raisings and husking bees on the frontier?

In practice, most participants do not think much about the credits they receive, and many hours go unreported. In fact, time banks provide a case study in the limitations of economic reasoning. Many participants are emphatic that they wouldn't do for money what they do for the satisfaction of helping. "I would be a lousy doctor," Herbie Fine says. "I wouldn't charge anybody nothing. I'd say, 'Call me anytime.' My name is Fine. I want to keep it fine."

19

Who Owns the Beach?

S ome 70 percent of the Earth's surface consists of oceans, and we all own them. But getting access to what we own isn't always easy.

Here's the math. Half the population of the United States lives within 50 miles of the coast. But 70 percent of coastal land is privately owned, and the percentage is increasing all the time. A relatively small group of private owners constitutes a blockade to a much larger group of common owners. What gives?

If this sounds like a cue for lawyers to enter—well, it is. Beachfront access has become a heated issue from California to Maine and in the Great Lakes states in between. There have been major victories for the public, but private property fundamentalists have mounted a predictable reaction, and the Supreme Court is not inhospitable to their cause.

Coastal access is one arena in which the weight of precedent stands on the commoners' side. The public trust doctrine, which goes back to Roman times, declares that waterways are inherently public and cannot be sold even if the sovereign wants to. The first U.S. court to articulate this doctrine was the New Jersey Supreme Court, in a case involving oyster beds. "Where the tide ebbs and flows, the ports, the bays, the coasts of the sea, including both the water and the land under the water . . . are common to all the people," the New Jersey court said in the nineteenth-century case of *Arnold v. Mundy*. Each person, it added, "has a right to use them according to his pleasure."

The U.S. Supreme Court embraced the doctrine in 1892 in *Illinois Central Railroad v. Illinois*, which involved an attempt by the Illinois legislature to transfer shoreline along Lake Michigan to the aforementioned railroad. Public trust lands are "held in trust for public uses," the Court said, and these uses are "always paramount." The railroad didn't get the land.

So far so good. But this still leaves the problem of private owners blocking access to waterfronts to begin with. What good does it do to own a beach if a wall of private houses stands in the way?

In California the math is especially thorny, as is the sociology. Some 80 percent of the state's residents live within an hour's drive of the ocean, and not a few of them have a yen for surf and sand. At the same time, there are famously wealthy people who own beachfront homes and are less than thrilled by people lounging or swimming below their decks. One surfer told the *New York Times* of a homeowner who tried to kick him off the beach. The man said "he did not like to look out his window and see people swimming, because it blocked his view," the surfer recalled.

Thirty years ago, California voters declared access to beaches a public right, and the state's Coastal Commission has been carrying out this mandate step by arduous step. Probably the most famous case involved David Geffen, the media big shot, who has a home in Malibu with a beachfront almost as long as a football field. Back in 1983, Geffen promised to provide public access through his land in exchange for permission to build servant quarters. Then he reneged, arguing that this would be a "taking" of his property without compensation. The case dragged on. Finally, Geffen relented.

Another access blocker has been Wendy McCaw, a billionaire and environmental donor who owns the Santa Barbara *News-Press* and whose beachfront in Santa Barbara County is 500 feet long. "There needs to be more effort toward protecting the embattled wildlife calling our beaches home," McCaw said, "rather than focusing on how to pack more humans with their destructive ways into those sensitive habitats." (And environmentalists wonder why a lot of people regard them as selfish elitists.)

But the Coastal Commission is pressing on. It banned no-trespassing signs and motorized beach patrols along Broad Beach in Malibu. Meanwhile, the New Jersey Supreme Court ordered a private beach club with a $700 seasonal membership fee to grant access to the public for $3 a day.

In the same spirit, the Michigan Supreme Court affirmed that the public has the right to stroll along the beach and that beachfront owners have no right to stop them. This opens up the state's 3,200 miles of Great Lakes shoreline to public use. Walking on the beach, the court said, is "inherent in the exercise of traditionally-protected rights." The decision did not address the question of access, only the right of use.

Certainly, property owners are entitled to rules that protect against egregious nuisances, such as noise, crowding, and trash. It's reasonable not to want boom boxes and beach parties behind one's house late into the night. (In Geffen's case, the public access path will be locked at night.) But common owners have rights too, and it is fitting that courts are recognizing that.

20

From Alleys to Commons

In Baltimore, inner-city neighbors are starting to close off alleys and turn them into protected commons for socializing and children's play. The move is an answer to a number of problems many city dwellers face. They don't know their neighbors. They feel confined in their apartments. Their children lack safe places to play. Crime flourishes in the social void.

But look out back. There's an alley running right through the interior of the block. Probably it is a mess. Drug dealers hang out there; junkies shoot up. It's not a place you like to spend time.

But it's space. What if you could fix it up, even turn it into a park? What if neighbors lowered their back fences and opened up their yards to the new space? What if they put gates at the ends, with locks, so that children could play safely, and neighbors could plant gardens and install benches without worries about intruders? Then, what if people on the block gave a portion of their backyards to the new commons to make it bigger? Each one would lose a little, but together they would gain so much.

Gee, do you suppose?

In fact there are alleys like this in several cities. In Baltimore, the idea took hold on a block in the Patterson Park neighborhood. With help from Community Greens, a project of the Ashoka Foundation, residents got permission from the city to gate an alley. Then they cleaned it up, installed painted planters, and held a big block party. The effort inspired the city council to make it easier for other blocks to follow suit.

In Boston's South End there is a new commons called Montgomery Park, which neighbors turned from a virtual dump into an urban oasis. On Stanton Street in Manhattan's Lower East Side there is a housing project that was designed with help from people in the community. They scrapped the typical model of buildings set on an exposed landscape and opted for one with an enclosed inner courtyard. Children now have a safe place to play in a neighborhood that was formerly a drug combat zone. Parents watch their children from kitchen windows and laundry rooms.

It might seem new but actually it is old—development to meet social needs and not those of real estate speculators. The Pilgrims built their townhouses close together and farmed fields on the outskirts. In Paris, many old apartment buildings are built around inner courtyards like the one on Stanton Street. In Little Italy in Manhattan, street-facing facades give no hint of the islands of serenity that lie within.

There is a similar model of enclosed serenity that gives some people pause: Gramercy Park, a gated New York block that is cooperatively owned but accessible only to residents of nearby buildings who have keys. Can an alley be a commons if it is not open to everyone? The alleys are city property, after all.

Finite commons require rules of access, and historically access has been defined locally. You couldn't just show up with a cow in colonial Boston and expect to graze it on the common; the common was for Boston residents only. This is how most commons have worked, and it is how the "tragedy" of the commons is averted.

Some urban spaces, such as Central Park in New York, can be open to all if they have heavy policing, but back alleys won't, and that's just the way things are. Why shouldn't inner-city residents be able to enjoy the peace and safety of an enclosed common space? Residences are exclusive, so why can't a group of them share exclusive space?

21

New Institutions Needed

The kind of social structure that makes commons productive in the Alps of Switzerland, the rice fields of the
Philippines, and many other settings are not always possible
in the United States. What's more, some commons—such as
the oceans and the atmosphere—are too large to be amenable
to participatory management. The challenge is to build formal institutions that replicate the essential features of commons even if they cannot include the social dynamic of local
settings.

One essential feature is equity. Commons serve all, either
equally or by a just distributional standard, subject to necessary rules for access and use. A second essential feature is inter-
generational responsibility. Corporations are programmed to
maximize gains for the quarter or year. Commons, properly
designed, are encoded to preserve assets for future generations.

There are times when government can manage commons
according to these rules. For example, Central Park functions admirably as a commons under city ownership. But

government ownership is not always possible or best. In the United States, continuing pressure on national forests and other public lands illustrates the vulnerability of ownership that is ultimately political. At the local level, there are similar pressures to invade public spaces with corporate sponsorships, advertising, and so on.

At present, the institution that best embodies commons functions is the trust. Trusts exist by definition to maintain an asset for their beneficiaries, future or present. They have all the outer protections of private property, but inside they can be designed for other than profit-maximizing ends. It is not surprising that this legal form has emerged as a way to graft multigenerational responsibility onto an economic system that is geared to short-term gain.

An example is the Pacific Forest Trust, which helps protect private forests in the western United States from clear-cutting and development. About four-fifths of U.S. forest land is privately owned, and some 1.5 million acres of this disappears each year. The Pacific Forest Trust helps slow this trend by acquiring conservation easements (development rights) and holding them in perpetuity without using them. Private owners get to keep their land and harvest it sustainably, while the public gets healthy forests for a fraction of what it would cost to buy them.

In similar fashion, the Marin Agricultural Land Trust (MALT) buys development rights to the rolling ranch lands in west Marin County, California. Ranchers get to keep and work their land and pass it on to heirs. The public gets unspoiled landscapes plus active stewards on the land. To date, MALT has protected nearly half the ranch land in the county.

These sorts of trusts—of which there are thousands—are mostly local or regional. The Nature Conservancy and the Trust for Public Land are national versions. The next challenge is to apply the trust model to larger commons such as the atmosphere and oceans. That is one of the aims of the sky trust proposal discussed earlier.

For decades we have been told that there are only two ways to manage natural resources: corporate profit-maximizing or government ownership. In fact there is a third option. Commons management has worked for centuries and is working today. It is especially good at the local level and can be adapted to the most pressing global problems, including climate change.

22

Seeds of a Commons Movement

Every movement requires a story. To claim the future it must first explain the past.

The true story of the commons does this. It explains how we lost the capacity to see our own wealth. It debunks the myth that privatization is always progress. And it shows how growth has become a form of cannibalism in which the market devours the bases of its own existence.

Many of us know this story at some level, but usually it is a story without a name or solution. The commons provides both: it is the commons that is being devoured and the commons that must be restored. What's more, it is the commons that opens the way to a politics outside the left/right divide.

Some on the right are starting to see that the market isn't the answer to every problem. Many on the left are coming to the same conclusion about government. So what's the alternative? An alternative potentially acceptable to both sides is the commons.

If one looks closely, one can see the seeds of a new commons movement germinating. They're visible in many places, from local land trusts to your laptop to your tabletop. They're seen in battles against Walmart, patented seeds, and advertising in schools, as well as in open source software, free wi-fi hot spots, farmers' markets, time banks, and big ideas like the sky trust.

Over the years, I've reported on many of these developments. And I've come to believe that these seemingly unrelated battles and institutions are, in fact, the beginnings of a new commons sector. Like those in soil, these seeds will grow with nurturance and support. If they get that support, a vibrant commons sector can, in time, protect nature, reduce inequality, and improve the quality of life for rich and poor alike.

A protected and enhanced commons requires three things. First, it needs institutions that effectively manage common wealth on behalf of future generations. Such institutions should be transparent, free of corporate influence, and legally accountable to future generations. Many existing trusts show how this can be done.

Second, it requires property rights. As capitalists know, property is power, and at this moment our common assets lack adequate property rights. Hence, they can be trespassed upon by private corporations almost at will. Common property needs to be shielded from such transgressions, just as private property is.

Third, a strengthened commons requires government support. This doesn't mean government ownership; the state and the commons are two different things. It means government nurturing the commons as zealously as it nurtures corporations—indeed more zealously, to make up for decades of neglect.

Since the commons is neither the market nor the state, its advocates aren't locked into traditional conservative or liberal camps. They can enlist the state the same way partisans of the market do—to establish rules and boundaries and protect property, in this case common property—and then let the game play out. The goal isn't to replace the market with the commons but to build a durable balance between the two on a level playing field.

It's a new kind of freedom movement, a fight for freedom not just from the state but from short-term profit obsession. If it catches on, the cause of freedom will take another turn.

AFTERWORD

By David Bollier

As Jonathan Rowe makes clear, the commons is more than an inventory of physical resources. It is first and foremost a social system that describes how we relate to each other and to resources essential to our lives. The privatization of shared resources is thus not simply a theft of our land, air, and culture; it is also an assault upon our humanity and identities.

Much of Jonathan's work was dedicated to exploring this uncharted realm. He wanted to name the realm and give it a proper account. His hope was that once we recognized the limits of markets and the value of commons, a more serious project of social reconstruction could begin.

The encouraging news is that many positive developments are underway. Elinor Ostrom's 2009 Nobel Prize in Economics helped neutralize the "tragedy of the commons" fable popularized by Garrett Hardin in his 1968 essay. At the same time, there has been an explosion of interest in the commons among cities, online communities, artists, environmentalists, food activists, indigenous peoples, academics, and others. At the global level, the World Social Forum pushed for commons recognition at the Rio+20 conference in 2012. And everywhere there is growing use of commons language and recognition of nonmonetized inputs and externalities that mainstream economists ignore.

Jonathan's great insight was to recognize the deep gravitational pull that the idea of the commons exerts on the human spirit. We gravitate to the commons because it speaks to our need for fairness and inclusion. Jonathan understood this, and it is why his book has such a strong undertow. He was speaking about something very old and enduring, yet also something very contemporary.

Jonathan properly saw the commons as a means both for reestablishing human connection and reinventing democracy. At a time when governments around the world are seen as inaccessible, incompetent, or corrupt, the commons allows people to take meaningful action where they stand, right now, without anyone's permission.

The theory of the commons clearly needs to evolve further, but when theory needs to catch up with practice, something powerful is going on. Jonathan Rowe was one of the first to grasp this reality and explain it in graceful words.

David Bollier is an author, activist, and independent scholar who studies the commons as a paradigm of political culture and economics. He is cofounder of the Commons Strategies Group, cofounder of Public Knowledge, and blogs at www.bollier.org.

NOTES

INTRODUCTION

1. Jonathan Rowe, Clifford Cobb, and Ted Halstead, "If the GDP Is Up, Why Is America Down?" *Atlantic Monthly*, October 1995. Available at www.theatlantic.com/past/politics/ecbig/gdp.htm.

2. Jonathan Rowe, "Rebuilding the Nonmarket Economy," *The American Prospect*, December 19, 2001. Available at http://prospect.org/article/rebuilding-nonmarket-economy.

3. Bill O'Reilly's and Lou Dobbs's exchange can be found at www.foxnews.com/on-air/oreilly/index.html#/v/1472237953001/government-intervention-in-the-american-oil-industry/?playlist_id=86923.

CHAPTER 1, OUR HIDDEN WEALTH

1. Edmund Burke, *Reflections on the French Revolution*, 1790.

CHAPTER 2, HOW TRAGIC IS THE COMMONS

1. Garrett Hardin, "The Tragedy of the Commons," *Science*, 1968, pp. 1243–1248. Available at www.sciencemag.org/content/162/3859/1243.full.pdf.

2. E. P. Thompson, *The Making of the English Working Class* (Gollancz, 1991).

3. See Elinor Ostrom's Nobel Lecture at www.nobelprize.org/nobel_prizes/economics/laureates/2009/ostrom-lecture.html.

4. David Harris, *The Last Stand: The War between Wall Street and Main Street over California's Ancient Redwoods* (Time Books/Random House, 1995).

CHAPTER 3, A NEW COMMONS STORY

1. Adam Smith, *An Inquiry into the Nature and Causes of the Wealth of Nations*, 1776.

CHAPTER 5, STOP THE INVASIONS!

1. Maude Barlow and Tony Clarke, *Blue Gold: The Fight to Stop the Corporate Theft of the World's Water* (New Press, 2002).

CHAPTER 7, HUMAN NATURE AND THE COMMONS

1. Learn about the Wikimedia Foundation, which develops and distributes free multilingual content to readers everywhere, at http://wikimediafoundation.org/wiki/Home.

2. U.S. Department of Agriculture data. See www.ams.usda.gov/AMSv1.0/ams.fetchTemplateData.do?template=TemplateS&leftNav=Wholesale andFarmersMarkets&page=WFMFarmersMarketGrowth&description =Farmers%20Market%20Growth&acct=frmrdirmkt.

CHAPTER 8, COMMON PROPERTY

1. Carol Rose, "The Comedy of the Commons: Commerce, Custom, and Inherently Public Property," *University of Chicago Law Review*, Summer 1986.

CHAPTER 9, TAKERS AND GIVERS

1. See Stuart Taylor Jr., "Does the President Agree with This Nominee?" *Atlantic Monthly*, May 2005. Available at www.theatlantic.com/magazine/archive/2005/05/does-the-president-agree-with-this-nominee/304012/.

2. Richard Epstein, *Simple Rules for a Complex World* (Harvard University Press, 1995).

CHAPTER 10, THE COMMUNITY OF GOODS

1. William Novak, *The People's Welfare: Law and Regulation in Nineteenth-Century America* (University of North Carolina Press, 1996), p. 72.

CHAPTER 11, CONSERVATIVE COMMONERS, ONCE

1. Russell Kirk, *The Conservative Mind: From Burke to Eliot* (Regnery, 1953), p. 121.

2. Ibid.

3. Wilhelm Ropke, *A Humane Economy: The Social Framework of the Free Market* (Regnery, 1960). Available at http://mises.org/books/Humane_Economy_Ropke.pdf.

4. http://mises.org/page/1461/Biography-of-Wilhelm-Ropke-18991966-Humane-Economist.

CHAPTER 12, ACCOUNTING FOR COMMON WEALTH

1. *The State of The Commons Report*, first published in 2003, can be found at http://onthecommons.org/sites/default/files/stateofthecommons.pdf. The editor of this book and the author of the afterword were coauthors of the report with Rowe.

2. www.munichre.com/en/media_relations/press_releases/2012/2012_10_17_press_release.aspx.

CHAPTER 13, TOLLBOOTHS OF THE MIND

1. Thomas Jefferson, letter to Isaac McPherson, August 13, 1813. Available at www.temple.edu/lawschool/dpost/mcphersonletter.html.

2. Benjamin Franklin, *The Autobiography of Benjamin Franklin* (Pater-Noster Row, 1771). Available at www.ushistory.org/franklin/autobiography/index.htm.

3. Jonas Salk's comment is from a CBS television interview on *See It Now* with Ed Murrow, April 12, 1955.

4. See list of McDonald's trademarks at www.mcdonalds.com/us/en/terms_conditions.html.

5. Lawrence Lessig, *The Future of Ideas: The Fate of the Commons in a Connected World* (Random House, 2001).

6. Ibid.

Chapter 14, Subsistence from the Commons

1. Steven Hahn, *The Roots of Southern Populism: Yeoman Farmers and the Transformation of the Georgia Upcountry* (Oxford University Press, 1983), p. 241.

Chapter 15, Build It and They Will Sit

1. William H. Whyte, *The Social Life of Small Urban Spaces* (Conservation Foundation, 1980), p. 19.

Chapter 16, Sidewalks of the Information Age

1. Jeff Gelles, "Digital Divide Still Wide in Philadelphia," *Philadelphia Inquirer*, March 29, 2012. Available at http://articles.philly.com/2012-03-29/news/31255078_1_national-broadband-plan-broadband-service-public-computer-centers.

Chapter 17, Reallocating Time

1. Robert Putnam, *Bowling Alone: The Collapse and Revival of American Community* (Touchstone Books, 2001), p. 27.

ACKNOWLEDGMENTS

This book could not have been written without the contributions over many years of people who knew, worked, and thought about things with Jonathan. I cannot possibly list all of these people here, but they most certainly include Alan AtKisson, Russ Baker, Harriet Barlow, Elizabeth Barnet, David Bollier, Clifford Cobb, Chuck Collins, Ann Depue, Byron Dorgan, James Fallows, Sarah van Gelder, Paul Glastris, John de Graaf, Lewis Hyde, Edgar Kahn, Mickey Kaus, Michael Kinsey, George Lakoff, Jim Lardner, Bill McKibben, David Morris, Ralph Nader, Jacob Needleman, Timothy Noah, Charlie Peters, John Richard, Julie Ristau, Gary Ruskin, Sam Smith, Tracy Wahl, and Jay Walljasper.

Jonathan's family supported him at all times, especially his brother Matthew Rowe, his wife Mary Jean Espulgar-Rowe, and his son Joshua Espulgar-Rowe.

The incredibly competent people at Berrett-Koehler, including Steve Piersanti, the publisher, and Jeevan Sivasubramaniam, the executive managing editor, made the book happen. Deep thanks are due to all.

Thanks are also due to the following for permission to adapt articles by Jonathan Rowe into this book: OnThe

Commons.org, *YES!* magazine, *Business Ethics*, the *Christian Science Monitor*, *Earth Island Journal*, The New Press, *Ode, Sierra, The American Prospect*, and the Worldwatch Institute.

— *Ed.*

INDEX

Index

genetic modification, 32, 65–66, 101

givings, 49–50

government

  and boundaries between the market and the commons, 16–17, 30

  compensation for private property taken by, 46

  invasion of the commons by, 20, 46

  management of the commons by, 97–98

  political debate on market versus, 15

  support for and protection of commons by, 45, 47, 60, 102

  takings theory and, 48–49

Great Britain. *See* England

Great Lakes, 91, 93

Grotius, Hugo, 52

growth. *See* economic growth

Gulf of Mexico, 61

H

Hahn, Steven, 69

Hansen, James, xi–xii

happiness, 3, 29, 40

Hardin, Garrett, xii, 11, 18–21, 25, 103

Harris, David, 21

health maintenance organizations (HMOs), 86–87

homo economicus, 39–40

Hughes, Ray, 88–89

human economy, 37–43

human nature, 37–43, 104

Humane Economy, A (Ropke), 55

hunting. *See* fishing and hunting

hurricanes, 49–51, 53, 62

Hurwitz, Charles, 22

hyperactivity, 26

I

Illinois Central Railroad v. Illinois, 91

income from common wealth, 7, 59, 71

income tax, 73. *See also* taxes

Industrial Revolution, 5, 27, 33, 85

Institutes of Natural Law (Rutherford), 51

intellectual property rights. *See* copyrights; patents

Internet

  broadband Internet access, 79–81

  corporations and, 16–17, 66

  low income families and, 79

  as part of the commons, 4, 11, 14, 49, 66

  wi-fi networks and, 6, 60, 79–81, 101

  Wikipedia and, 37–38, 41, 43

inventions. *See* patents

irrigation, 19, 61. *See also* agriculture

Index

Index

ABOUT THE AUTHOR

JONATHAN ROWE was born in 1946 in a small town outside of Boston, Massachusetts. A 1967 graduate of Harvard College, he earned a law degree from the University of Pennsylvania and in the early 1970s was one of Ralph Nader's original "Raiders." Later he served on staffs in the U.S. House of Representatives and Senate, where he was a longtime aide to Senator Byron Dorgan (D-North Dakota). He was a contributing editor to the *Washington Monthly* and *YES!* magazines, a staff writer for the *Christian Science Monitor*, and a contributor to *Harper's*, the *Atlantic Monthly*, the *Columbia Journalism Review*, and many other publications. In addition, he cofounded the Tomales Bay Institute, On The Commons, and West Marin Commons. He died unexpectedly on March 20, 2011.

Hundreds of Jonathan Rowe's writings—including those incorporated in this book—are collected at www.jonathanrowe.org. The site also includes audio files taken from his weekly radio show on KWMR.

ABOUT THE EDITOR

PETER BARNES is an entrepreneur and writer who started several successful businesses, including Working Assets/Credo. He has written for *Newsweek*, the *New Republic*, and numerous other magazines, and is the author of five books, including *Who Owns the Sky?* and *Capitalism 3.0*. He cofounded the Tomales Bay Institute with Jonathan Rowe, and founded The Mesa Refuge, a writer's retreat in Point Reyes Station, on whose board Rowe served for ten years.

ABOUT ON THE COMMONS

ON THE COMMONS, the successor organization to the Tomales Bay Institute, was cofounded in 2001 by Jonathan Rowe, who also served as its first director. Its purpose is to assist and bring visibility to people who are defending and expanding the commons.

Now based in Minneapolis, On The Commons has published numerous articles and reports, initiated several campaigns and demonstration projects, and promoted commons thinking worldwide. Its website, www.onthecommons.org, is a lively online magazine for commons theory and work. Much of this book first appeared there.

ABOUT WEST MARIN COMMONS

WEST MARIN COMMONS, based in Point Reyes Station, California, was cofounded in 2006 by Jonathan Rowe to enhance commons practice in west Marin County. Among other things, it has built a public native plant garden, an informal town commons, and a website for sharing free stuff. For more information visit www.westmarincommons.org.

Berrett–Koehler
Publishers

Berrett-Koehler is an independent publisher dedicated to an ambitious mission: *Creating a World That Works for All.*

We believe that to truly create a better world, action is needed at all levels—individual, organizational, and societal. At the individual level, our publications help people align their lives with their values and with their aspirations for a better world. At the organizational level, our publications promote progressive leadership and management practices, socially responsible approaches to business, and humane and effective organizations. At the societal level, our publications advance social and economic justice, shared prosperity, sustainability, and new solutions to national and global issues.

A major theme of our publications is "Opening Up New Space." Berrett-Koehler titles challenge conventional thinking, introduce new ideas, and foster positive change. Their common quest is changing the underlying beliefs, mindsets, institutions, and structures that keep generating the same cycles of problems, no matter who our leaders are or what improvement programs we adopt.

We strive to practice what we preach—to operate our publishing company in line with the ideas in our books. At the core of our approach is stewardship, which we define as a deep sense of responsibility to administer the company for the benefit of all of our "stakeholder" groups: authors, customers, employees, investors, service providers, and the communities and environment around us.

We are grateful to the thousands of readers, authors, and other friends of the company who consider themselves to be part of the "BK Community." We hope that you, too, will join us in our mission.

A BK Currents Book

This book is part of our BK Currents series. BK Currents books advance social and economic justice by exploring the critical intersections between business and society. Offering a unique combination of thoughtful analysis and progressive alternatives, BK Currents books promote positive change at the national and global levels. To find out more, visit **www.bkconnection.com**.

Berrett–Koehler
Publishers

A community dedicated to creating
a world that works for all

Visit Our Website: www.bkconnection.com

Read book excerpts, see author videos and Internet movies, read
our authors' blogs, join discussion groups, download book apps, find
out about the BK Affiliate Network, browse subject-area libraries of
books, get special discounts, and more!

Subscribe to Our Free E-Newsletter, the *BK Communiqué*

Be the first to hear about new publications, special discount offers,
exclusive articles, news about bestsellers, and more! Get on the list
for our free e-newsletter by going to **www.bkconnection.com**.

Get Quantity Discounts

Berrett-Koehler books are available at quantity discounts for orders
of ten or more copies. Please call us toll-free at (800) 929-2929 or
email us at bkp.orders@aidcvt.com.

Join the BK Community

BKcommunity.com is a virtual meeting place where people from
around the world can engage with kindred spirits to create a world
that works for all. **BKcommunity.com** members may create their own
profiles, blog, start and participate in forums and discussion groups,
post photos and videos, answer surveys, announce and register for
upcoming events, and chat with others online in real time. Please join
the conversation!

MIX
Paper from
responsible sources
FSC® C012752